Home Sweet Home
AN EMBROIDERED WORKBOX

Carolyn Pearce

AUTHOR	Carolyn Pearce
EDITOR	Anna Scott
ASSISTANT EDITOR	Jessica Marshallsay
EDITORIAL TEAM	Ellaine Bronsert, Heidi Reid
ILLUSTRATIONS & DIAGRAMS	Kathleen Barac
PATTERN DESIGN	Kathleen Barac
GRAPHIC DESIGN	Lynton Grandison, Fabrizia Conteria
PHOTOGRAPHY	ADP

First published 2011 in Australia by Country Bumpkin Publications

Second edition in 2013 by Inspirations Books

Third edition and updated in 2016 by Inspirations Studios

Inspirations Studios
PO Box 10177
Adelaide Business Centre
South Australia 5000
info@inspirationsstudios.com
www.inspirationsstudios.com

Copyright © Inspirations Studios Corporation 2016

National Library of Australia Cataloguing-in-Publication entry
Pearce, Carolyn.
Home sweet home : an embroidered workbox / Carolyn Pearce.
9780980876703 (pbk.)
Embroidery. Needlework.
746.44

Disclaimer
Information and instructions given in this book are presented in good
faith, but no warranty is given nor results guaranteed, nor is freedom from
any patent to be inferred. As we have no control over physical conditions
surrounding application of information herein contained in this book, the
author and publisher disclaim any liability for untoward results.

CONTENTS

The Embroidered Workbox

BY CAROLYN PEARCE

One day as a reward at school I was given a needlework leaflet for an embroidered box that opened on the top. How I longed to make that box! Sadly, over the years I lost the leaflet, although I still have my carefully handwritten notes on how to work the various stitches.

Then one day, flicking through an English magazine, I saw a picture of an antique sycamore doll's house workbox, dated to 1780. It was described as having 'a baize bottom and apple-green lining paper. Inside is a detachable tray with tiny compartments for cottons and threads as well as a secret side drawer that is secured with a peg'. Immediately my imagination was sparked.

First, I built the box out of cardboard and sticky tape. The construction was inspired by the numerous Japanese paper covered boxes I have made over the years. I also drew on Jane Lemon's books on boxmaking, as well as Jackie Woosey's *Making Hand-Sewn Boxes.*

Particularly valuable was a workshop with Nola Moran on box making.

Once I'd worked out the construction of the box, I drew the embroidery designs on paper and taped them to each panel. I always knew I wanted a whimsical Elizabethan-inspired garden, so I included lots of field flowers and grasses on each panel. Then the fun part – choosing colours and threads!

When I was close to finishing my workbox, I went to a talk by Genevieve Cummins about her new book, *Antique Boxes: Inside and Out.* This inspired me to make matching needlework accessories. Another few months of work! While I was making them, I thought it was a pity the tray did not have compartments. The tray had been such an angst-filled project, getting it to fit snugly inside the box, I was horrified at the thought of taking it apart! Finally, after winning a prize for the workbox, I was in the right frame of mind to take it apart and add the dividers.

I have seen several finished workboxes, some with their own special touches. One inspiration was the workbox made by Thelma Hunt, a retired pathologist in her 80s. She brought her box to one of my classes, complete with a beautifully embroidered base. At that stage, my box only had a plain base, but spurred on by Thelma's example I took my box apart yet again, and added embroidery to the base.

I made my box in 2007, and since then have taught it to many people. Now I am thrilled to share the designs with you in this book.

Carolyn

In memory of Sandra Denise Ricketts (1944–2010), whose beautiful embroidered workbox is treasured by her family.

How to use this book

Home Sweet Home has all the information you need to create your very own embroidered house workbox. The first half of the book contains the embroidery techniques and construction methods for the box. The second half of the book contains the instructions for the accessories. This gives you many options for creating the beautiful embroidery in this book. You can follow the book through from beginning to end to create the complete workbox and all its accessories, or you can just pick your favourite accessories to embroider.

We recommend that you read the complete instructions for the embroidery relating to each section of the box and accessories before you begin.

You can customise the box and accessories; perhaps you could add some beautiful beads, buttons and charms, or maybe even choose your favourite flowers and animals to add to the embroidery.

The finished workbox measures 16cm high x 15.5cm long x 9.8cm wide (6 5/16" x 6 1/8" x 3 7/8").

House Box

Requirements

Fabric

30cm x 146cm wide (12" x 58") natural cotton–linen blend (walls and base)

50cm x 115cm wide (20" x 46") pale butter and fern green print cotton (lining and tray)

25cm (10") square of dusty green Permin linen (roof)

10cm (4") square of 14-count waste canvas (front door)

50cm x 112cm wide (20" x 44") calico (waste fabric)

15cm (6") square of crystal organza (windows)

40cm x 90cm wide (16" x 36") piece of white felt (padding)

3cm x 6cm wide (1¼" x 2⅜") piece of red wool felt (strawberries)

3cm x 10cm wide (1¼" x 4") piece of light brown wool felt (orange basket, snail shell)

Supplies

20cm (8") square of appliqué paper (windows, tray dividers)

30cm (12") square of lightweight non-woven interfacing (pattern pieces)

30cm x 5mm wide (12" x ³⁄₁₆") length of elastic

4 x 6mm (¼") pearl buttons

4 x 14mm (⁹⁄₁₆") self-cover buttons with linen shank

Fine grey beading thread, e.g. Nymo

Clear nylon thread

Machine sewing threads to match fabrics

Quilting thread

10cm x 15cm wide (4" x 6") piece of lightweight fusible interfacing

56cm x 82cm wide (22" x 33") piece of 2mm (⅛") cream or white acid-free mountboard (workbox sides, base, roof and risers, tray sides)

10cm (4") square of 1.5mm (¹⁄₁₆") cream or white acid-free mountboard (tray dividers)

Tiger Tape, 9 lines/inch

HINT
Tiger Tape

Tiger Tape is a white self-adhesive tape used by quilters. The ¼"-wide tape has evenly spaced black lines printed across its width and is available in 4, 9, or 12 lines per inch.

Beads & Charms

1 x 4mm (³⁄₁₆") brass coloured disc spacer bead (door handle)

2 x 7mm (⁵⁄₁₆") green nephrite cylinder beads (chimney)

2 x 4mm (³⁄₁₆") brown round beads (chimney)

18mm (¾") flowerpot charm (front wall)

3 x 10mm (³⁄₈") brass bees (strawberry end wall)

15mm (⁵⁄₈") brass beehive button (strawberry end wall)

Susan Clarke Originals

Beehive – 720 (back wall)

✓ Carrot – 740 (front wall)

✓ Gecko – 867 (pea end wall)

✓ Ladybird – C-107 (pea end wall)

✓ Owl – BE-78 (back wall)

✓ Rabbit – 236 (back wall)

Equipment

20cm (8") deep sided embroidery hoop, inner ring bound

¼"-inch press bar (optional)

Loop turner (optional)

Dressmaker's awl or stiletto

Berry pins

Cutting mat

Sharp craft knife

Set square

Metal ruler

PVA glue

Beeswax (optional)

Fine sandpaper

Baking paper

Tracing paper

Mechanical pencil

Fine black pen

Fine 01 (0.25mm) brown permanent acid-free pen, e.g. Pigma or Zig

Needles

See page 10.

Threads, Beads & Sequins

See page 11.

HINT
Embroidery hoop

I prefer to use a deep sided round hoop. Excess fabric can be rolled up with the embroidery facing inwards and the end of the roll secured to the sides with small safety pins.

Preparation for embroidery

See the liftout pattern for the embroidery designs. All seam allowances are 2.5cm (1") unless otherwise specified.

Cutting out

Referring to the cutting layout, cut the cotton–linen fabric into five panels for the walls and base.

Natural cotton–linen blend

Base: cut one, 18cm x 25.5cm wide (7" x 10")

Front and back walls: cut two, each 20.5cm x 25.5cm wide (8" x 10")

End wall: cut two, each 25.5cm x 18cm wide (10" x 7")

Preparing the fabric

Using the black pen, trace the dashed lines of the base and two wall templates onto the lightweight interfacing and cut out.

Centre the long wall template over a corresponding cotton–linen piece, aligning the lower edge with the straight grain of the fabric, and pin in place.

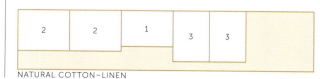

NATURAL COTTON–LINEN

Natural cotton–linen blend
1. Base
2. Front and back walls
3. End walls

Tack around the outline of the shape using pale machine sewing thread. Repeat for the remaining long wall piece and end walls. Tack two rectangles, each 6.5cm x 16cm wide (2½" x 6¼") for the roof onto the olive-green evenweave, spacing the pieces 6cm (2⅜") apart. Cut the evenweave in half between the two tacked lines.

Neaten the raw edges of all the pieces with an overlock or machine zigzag stitch to prevent fraying. Cut the piece of calico into 10cm (4") wide strips. Using a machine zigzag, stitch calico strips to all four sides of one piece so that it will fit into the hoop (diag 1).

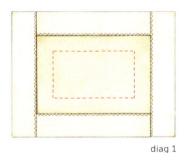

diag 1

Repeat for the remaining four pieces and the two evenweave roof pieces.

Transferring the designs

Using the fine black pen, trace the embroidery designs and cutting lines for the front and back walls, end walls and base onto separate pieces of tracing paper. Use the alphabet supplied for your name on the base. Mark the centres of the flowers with a dot and the positions of the buttons and charms with a cross.

Position a back wall tracing onto a lightbox or window and tape in place. With the right side facing up, place a corresponding fabric piece over the tracing, aligning the tacked outlines with the dashed lines, and tape in place. Using the fine brown permanent pen, lightly trace the design and cutting lines onto the fabric, omitting the outline for the fly stitch leaves.

Repeat for the remaining three sides and base.

General instructions

Embroidery

All embroidery is worked with the fabric held taut in the hoop using the needle in a stabbing motion, except the fly stitch leaves and rosette flowers.

All embroidery is worked with one strand unless otherwise specified. When using more than one strand of cotton, silk or wool, separate the strands and then put them back together.

Where possible, work with the grain of the thread. The grain of the thread usually follows the direction the thread is pulled from the skein or reel, so it's best to thread the old end (rather than the freshly cut end) of thread through the eye of the needle.

It is important to secure your stitches at the beginning and end of your work. One method is to start with two tiny back stitches in the area to be embroidered, splitting the first stitch with the second. Finish with two tiny back stitches on the wrong side of the work. If there is nowhere to conceal the starting point, start with a waste knot around 5cm (2") from where the first stitch will be placed, and finish by securing the thread under the stitching on the wrong side.

Also make sure not to carry thread long distances on the back of the work, as this may show through on the front. It is better to end off and start again.

When working eyelets for attaching charms, hold the charm in position and mark a 4–5mm (³⁄₁₆–¼") circle at the position for the shank.

Construction

Construct one section of the box at a time before moving on to the next, working from the outside in. This will allow you to adjust your measurements as you go for accurate construction.

CUTTING THE MOUNTBOARD

Accuracy is important when measuring and cutting the mountboard. Always use a set square, metal ruler and a sharp craft knife. It is useful to have spare blades for the craft knife.

When each piece is cut out, gently sand any rough edges with the piece of fine sandpaper.

1. Determine the grain. Gently bend the mountboard horizontally and then vertically. The direction in which it bends easiest is the direction of the grain. Mark the grain with a small arrow in the upper left corner.

2. Mark the mountboard. Use a set square to mark a right-angled corner in the upper right corner (fig 1).

fig 1

3. Measure the required size of the mountboard piece, using the right-angled corner as your reference. Double check all measurement and corners using the ruler and set square.

4. Cutting. Place a metal ruler along the cutting line over the piece to be cut and press down with the full length of your fingers and thumb.

5. Using a sharp craft knife, cut along the metal ruler. Make a number of small cuts, rather than trying to cut the line with one long cut (fig 2).

fig 2

6. Repeat for the remaining lines, rotating the piece for each cut and placing the ruler over the piece to be cut to avoid accidentally cutting into the piece.

Stitches

Detailed step-by-step instructions for uncommon stitches are provided on pages 83–99.
For other stitches please see a stitch guide such as A–Z of Embroidery Stitches.

Armenian edging stitch
Attaching sequins
Back stitch
Beaded Hedebo edge
Beading
Blanket stitch
Bullion knot
Chain stitch
Cloud-filling stitch
Colonial knot
Coral stitch
Corded coral stitch
Couching
Cretan stitch variation
Cross stitch

Detached chain
Feather stitch
Fishbone stitch
Fly stitch
French knot
Ghiordes knot
Granitos
Heavy chain stitch
Hungarian braided chain stitch
Interlaced chain stitch
Knotted pearl stitch
Lacing
Ladder stitch
Long-armed cross stitch

Long and short stitch
Needlewoven picot
Outline stitch
Overcast stitch
Padded satin stitch
Pistil stitch
Portuguese border stitch
Portuguese knotted stem stitch
Raised chain band
Raised cross stitch
Raised stem band
Rococo stitch variation
Rosette stitch
Running stitch

Satin stitch
Seed stitch
Split back stitch
Stem stitch
Straight stitch
Threaded satin stitch honeycomb
Trellis stitch
Twisted chain stitch
Up and down blanket stitch loop
Whipping
Woven filling stitch

Needle chart

Needle	Thread	Number of strands	Stitch	Item
No. 9 betweens	Metallic	1–2		
No. 5 crewel	Fine wool No. 8 perlé cotton Stranded cotton or silk	1–2 1 4 or more		
No. 8 crewel	Stranded cotton or silk Wildflowers perlé cotton	3 1	Colonial knot	
No. 9 crewel	Stranded cotton or silk	2		
No. 10 crewel	Stranded cotton or silk Machine sewing thread	1 1	Ladder stitch	Mitring corners
No. 10 curved	Machine sewing thread	1	Ladder stitch	Constructing the box, needlebook
No. 5 milliner's	Stranded cotton	3	Bullion knot	Small caterpillar
No. 7 milliner's	No. 8 perlé cotton	1	Lacing	Pincushion
No. 22 tapestry	Variegated rayon/cotton No.5 perlé cotton	2 2	Threaded satin stitch honeycomb	Roof
No. 26 tapestry	Stranded cotton	2 1 2 1 2	Raised chain band Raised stem band Cloud-filling stitch Portugese border stitch Trellis stitch	Snail Snail, caterpillar Window Window Bee

Threads

Butterfly Thread

Au Papillon Fil d'Or deluxe — metallic "best"
A = medium gold ✓
B = dark gold

Au Ver à Soie Antique Metallics
C = 210 black copper ✓
D = 901 dk antique gold

Au Ver à Soie, Soie d'Alger — silk
E = 1342 lt antique violet
F = 1343 antique violet
G = 2214 med khaki green
H = 4147 vy lt blush
I = 4913 jacaranda blue
J = F15 lt old gold
K = Brut

Caron Soie Cristale stranded silk
L = 2031 dk brown rose
M = 2032 med brown rose
N = 2033 brown rose
O = 5022 dk olive green
P = 5023 olive green
Q = 5024 lt olive green

Caron Wildflowers perlé cotton
R = 031 rose quartz

Colour Streams Silken Strands
S = 23 rose blush
T = 25 Umbrian gold
U = 26 Tuscan olive
V = 37 Uluru

DMC no. 5 perlé cotton
W = 935 vy dk avocado green

DMC no. 8 perlé cotton
X = 469 avocado green

DMC no. 4 soft cotton
Y = 2013 lt khaki green

DMC stranded cotton
Z = 223 lt shell pink
AA = 310 black ✓
AB = 317 pewter grey
AC = 327 vy dk lavender

AD = 612 med taupe
AE = 712 cream
AF = 792 dk cornflower blue
AG = 839 chocolate
AH = 3012 med khaki green
AI = 3051 dk green-grey
AJ = 3052 med green-grey

Gloriana Lorikeet stranded wool
AK = 012W3 med rosewood
AL = 046W4 dk fallen leaves ✓
AM = 133W4 dk pecan

Gumnut Yarns 'Daisies' fine wool
AN = 865 med flesh
AO = 867 dk flesh
AP = 947 dk hazelnut ✓
AQ = 963 lt chocolate dip

Gumnut Yarns 'Stars' stranded silk
AR = 606 med dk rainforest
AS = 646 med dk khaki ✓
AT = 859 ultra dk salmon pink
AU = 998 vy dk pewter

Madeira stranded silk
AV = 0901 lt blue-violet
AW = 0902 blue-violet

Rajmahal stranded rayon
AX = 374 realgar red
AY = 421 green earth

Scansilk 100% rayon machine thread
AZ = 1195 purple

The Gentle Art Sampler Threads
BA = 0311 holly berry ✓
BB = 1030 banker's grey

Threadworx stranded variegated cotton
BC = 1028 wet clay ✓

Weeks Dye Works stranded cotton
BD = 1246 sage ✓
BE = 2200 kudzu

YLI silk floss
BF = 7 vy lt antique mauve
BG = 157 olive green

BH = 188 antique mauve
BI = 191 ultra dk antique violet

Gumnut Yarns 'Buds' perlé silk
BJ = 645 (dk khaki)

YLI fine metallic
BK = gold 1

Beads & Sequins

Maria George Delica
BL = DBR 150 silver lined brown

Mill Hill seed beads
BM = 00221 bronze
BN = 02093 opaque autumn

Mill Hill petite seed beads
BO = 40556 antique silver
BP = 42037 green velvet

Non-branded craft beads & sequins
BQ = 5mm (3/16") blue flower beads
BR = 2mm (1/16") green sequins

11

Winter Rose

FRONT WALL

English cottage gardens are always associated with roses, so this climbing rose seemed the perfect feature for the front wall. The drawing for the rabbit is from *Designs from Historic Textiles* by Jan Messent, and the cornflower from *4000 Flower and Plant Motifs: A Source Book* by Graham Leslie McCallum.

THREADS & BEADS

Refer to the combined list of threads on page 11.

Au Papillon Fil d'Or deluxe
A

Au Ver à Soie, Soie d'Alger
E, F, G, I, J

Caron Soie Cristale stranded silk
L, M, N, O

Colour Streams Silken Strands
S, V

DMC stranded cotton
AA, AB, AC, AD, AE, AF, AH

Gloriana Lorikeet stranded wool
AK, AL, AM

Gumnut 'Daisies' fine wool
AN, AO, AP, AQ

Gumnut 'Stars' stranded silk
AR, AS, AU

Madeira stranded silk
AV, AW

Scansilk 100% rayon machine thread
AZ

The Gentle Art Sampler Threads
BB

Weeks Dye Works stranded cotton
BD

Beads

Mill Hill seed beads
BM

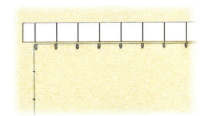

Embroidery

Follow the general embroidery instructions on page 9. Refer to the close-up photograph and embroidery key for colour placement, and the needle chart on page 10 for the use of needles.

Order of work

WINDOWS

Refer to the step-by-step instructions for cloud-filling stitch on page 84 and Portuguese border stitch on page 93.

Using the pencil and ruler, trace the windows for the front wall onto appliqué paper. Place a sheet of baking paper onto your ironing board. With the paper side facing, fuse the appliqué paper to the wrong side of the organza, placing a second sheet of baking paper on top to protect your iron.

Cut out the windows exactly on the pencil line. Peel off the paper backing and fuse the windows into position, protecting your iron and board with baking paper as before.

Panes

The leadlight for the window panes is embroidered in cloud-filling stitch.

Using the ruler and fine pencil, lightly mark 5mm (³⁄₁₆") intervals down one side of a window.

Place a strip of Tiger Tape along the upper edge of the organza. Bringing the needle to the front through the background fabric at the edge of the window and to the back just inside the edge of the organza, work tiny vertical straight stitches 3mm (¹⁄₈") apart using two strands of AB for the foundation of the cloud-filling stitch (*diag 2*).

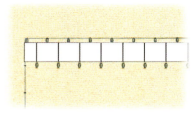

diag 2

Move the tape down to align with the first 5mm (³⁄₁₆") mark and work the next row of foundation stitches in a brick pattern (*diag 3*).

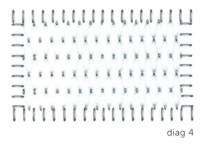

diag 3

Continue to work rows of foundation stitches in a brick pattern in this manner to the lower edge of the window, starting and finishing the rows at the edges of the organza.

Using two strands of BB in a tapestry needle, lace the diamond pattern into the foundation stitches. Avoid pulling the weaving thread too tight, as this will distort the shape of the diamonds.

Frame

The window frame is embroidered in Portuguese border stitch.

Using AU, work foundation stitches around the window each 2mm (¹⁄₁₆") long and approximately 3mm (¹⁄₈") apart. Bring the needle to the front a short distance from the edge of the window and take it to the back just inside the edge of the organza. Ensure that there is one stitch exactly at each corner and one 3mm (¹⁄₈") past each corner. The foundation stitches should be aligned on each side of the window (*diag 4*).

diag 4

Starting at the lower left hand corner and using the same thread in the no. 26 tapestry needle, lace into the foundation stitches.

Referring to diagram 5 for the starting points and direction of lacing, lace each end, then the upper edge of the window in the same manner.

Mullion

Using two strands of AU, work a row of chain stitch along the centre row of diamonds for the smaller windows. Divide the large window into three even widths and work two rows of chain stitch in a similar manner (*diag 5*).

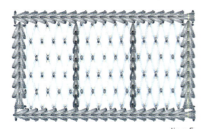

diag 5

Using two strands of the same thread in a tapestry needle, whip each row of chain stitch.

CLIMBING ROSE

Refer to the step-by-step instructions for working rosette stitch on page 96.

Vine

Beginning at the base, embroider the trunk in twisted chain stitch, using two strands of AL.

Work the branches in stem stitch using one strand of the same thread. To stitch the wider sections of the branches, work a row of outline stitch part way along the stem stitch, tucking the last stitch under the previous row to achieve a smooth join (*diag 6*).

diag 6

Leaves

All the leaves are embroidered in the same manner, using two strands of G, AH or AS. Beginning at the tip, stitch an uneven fly stitch – short on one side, long on the other. For a leaf

curving to the left, bring the thread to the front at (a), take it to the back at (b) and emerge at (c) to anchor the stitch (*diag 7*).

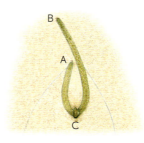

diag 7

For a leaf curving to the right, (a) should be above (b) (*diag 8*).

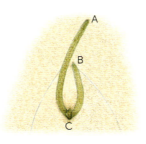

diag 8

Work fly stitches close together, gradually increasing the width of the stitches to shape the leaf. When the leaf is broad enough, gradually decrease the width of the stitches.

The anchoring stitches should line up neatly to make the mid rib of the leaf (*diag 9*).

diag 9

HINTS

Fly stitch leaves

1. I like to have points (a), (b) and (c) in a straight line and the distance from (a) to (b) equal to the distance from (b) to (c).

These proportions work well regardless of what thread I use.

2. Sometimes I tuck the last few fly stitches slightly underneath the previous stitch to keep a nice shape. It usually only takes a couple of stitches to round off the base of the leaf.

Roses

Using three strands of N or S, embroider a rosette stitch for each rose, finishing each with a colonial knot in the centre using the same thread.

HEARTSEASE

Petals

Referring to the diagram, outline petals one and two in split back stitch using E. Outline petals three and four using J, and petal five using F in the same manner (*diag 10*).

diag 10

Using the same threads, work one layer of padding within the outlines of petals one, three and four. Work two layers of padding within the outlines of the remaining two petals, ensuring the uppermost layer is worked across each shape. Cover the petals with satin stitch, angling the stitches towards the centre of the flower. To avoid bulk, work some stitches a little shorter, tucking them under the stitches on either side to achieve a smooth finish.

Add three straight stitch highlights on petals three and four using AZ, and five stitches on petal five. Change to two strands of T and work a colonial knot for the flower centre.

Stem and leaves

Stitching from the base of the flower, embroider the stem in heavy chain stitch using two strands of AR.

Outline the leaf with very small split back stitches using one strand of the same thread. Embroider the outer edge of the leaf in long and short stitch. Work each stitch from inside the leaf and over the outline, angling the stitches towards the base. Gradually change the angle of the stitches to indicate the direction of the veins. Change to O and work the inner section in long and short stitch, splitting the previous stitches. Embroider the centre vein in stem stitch using one strand of G.

Embroider the second leaf in the same manner.

HINT

Leaf – stitch direction

I prefer to start in the middle of one side of the leaf and work towards the stalk end. I then pass my thread under the stitches on the back and start working towards the tip, gradually tilting the stitches over so that at the tip they are parallel to the centre vein.

CORNFLOWER

Using two strands of AW and starting on the outer edge of the flower, work straight stitches at differing angles, each approximately 5mm (³/₁₆") in length. Change to I and work a second round in a similar manner, tucking the ends of the stitches under those of the previous row (diag 11).

diag 11

Work a third round inside the first using two strands of AV and blending the stitches into the previous rounds. Radiating from the centre, fill the flower with seed stitch using two strands of thread, changing between AC and AF. Add straight stitch highlights using A.

Stem and leaves

Embroider the stem in the same manner as the heartsease using two strands of AH.

Outline the leaves in split back stitch using BD. Using the same thread, fill each leaf with long and short stitch, covering the outline.

RABBIT

Partially outline the rabbit in split back stitch as shown, using AP (diag 12).

Head

Using AA, outline the eye with tiny split back stitch, then add a couple of satin stitches at the front of the eye for the pupil. Embroider small straight stitches, radiating around the eye, with AQ (diag 13).

diag 12

diag 13

Embroider the right hand ear in long and short stitch using AM, stitching from the top of the head towards the tip. Use a darker section of the thread closest to the left hand ear.

Stitch the left hand ear in a similar manner using AP. Add a few stitches using AN in the middle, blending them into the previous stitches.

Working from the nose towards the ears and covering the outlines, embroider the head with long and short stitch using AP.

Embroider a couple of tiny satin stitches for the nose with AN (diag 14).

diag 14

Body

Embroider the left paw in satin stitch using AM. Stitching from the shoulder to the paw, work the right foreleg in close rows of split back stitch with AP, covering the outlines and placing the darker sections of the thread along the upper edge of the leg.

Starting at the neck, fill the back with split back stitch using AP. Work a small area of satin stitch for the top of the shoulder using the same thread. Changing to AQ, work a few satin stitches under the chin. Fill the tummy in the same manner.

Embroider the left back foot in satin stitch with AM, and the right back foot with AP. Work the thigh in split back stitch using AP, altering the direction of the stitches to follow the shape.

Tail

Using AQ, work four rows of three tiny Ghiordes knots very close together. For the last row, have the thread above the line of work, so that the loops will hide the little back stitches.

HINTS *Long and short stitch*

There are a few important things to remember to achieve a good result:

1. Avoid making your stitch length too short.

2. Short stitches are ²/₃ as long as the long stitches.

3. On the first row, bring the thread to the front inside the shape, and take the needle to the back, just outside the outline. On second and subsequent rows bring the needle to the front, splitting the previous stitch by about a third of the length.

DOOR

Refer to the step-by-step instructions for working the Cretan stitch variation on page 85.

Cut a 7cm x 5cm wide (2¾" x 2") rectangle of waste canvas. Carefully tack it in place over the position for the door, aligning the grain of the fabric with the marked outline.

Work four vertical rows of Cretan stitch variation with AO, each row over 34 horizontal fabric threads. To achieve a straight lower edge, fill in the canvas with straight stitches, maintaining the same angle as the Cretan stitches. Carefully withdraw the threads of the canvas with the eye end of a needle.

Embroider two parallel rows of stem stitch for the door frame using AK. Using the fine beading thread, attach the brass coloured spacer bead with a seed bead (BM) for the handle.

HINT

Cretan stitch variation

I recommend that you work a small sample first to determine the stitch tension. If the stitches are not firm enough, they will be untidy when the canvas threads are withdrawn.

FIELD FLOWERS AND GRASS

Refer to the step-by-step instructions for raised cross stitch on page 95.

Grass

Using two strands of AH or BE, work straight stitches of differing lengths and angles 5mm (³⁄₁₆") from the lower tacked line. To lessen the risk of

puckering and decrease the amount of thread on the back, work the stitches as shown (*diag 15*).

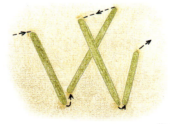

diag 15

Pink anemones

Referring to the close-up photograph for colour placement, work a raised cross stitch at the position of each flower, using two strands of L or M. Work a colonial knot at the centre of each flower using two strands of AA.

Cream daisies

Stitch three detached chains for the petals with two strands of AE, working the centre stitch first. Work a colonial knot in V for the flower centre.

Blue forget-me-nots

Using two strands of I, stitch a granitos for each petal. For each granitos work three stitches into the same holes. Leave a tiny space in the centre (*diag 16*).

diag 16

Change to two strands of V and work a colonial knot for the flower centre.

Using I, stitch pairs of colonial knots among the flowers for the tiny buds.

EYELETS AND CHARMS

Refer to the step-by-step instructions for working eyelets on page 86.

Use AD to stitch the eyelet and attach the charms. Stitch an eyelet at the position for the flowerpot charm next to the door and secure the charm.

Stitch the carrot charm in place between the rabbit's paws.

EMBROIDERY KEY

All embroidery is worked using one strand of thread unless otherwise specified.

Windows

Panes = AB (2 strands, straight stitch), BB (2 strands, lacing)

Frame = AU (Portuguese border stitch)

Mullion = AU (2 strands, chain stitch, whipping)

Climbing rose

Vine = AL (2 strands, twisted chain stitch, 1 strand, stem stitch, outline stitch)

Leaves = G, AH or AS (2 strands, fly stitch)

Roses = N or S (3 strands, rosette stitch, colonial knot)

Heartsease

Petals = E, F or J (split back stitch, padded satin stitch), AZ (straight stitch)

Centre = T (2 strands, colonial knot)

Stem = AR (2 strands, heavy chain stitch)

Leaves = AR (split back stitch, long and short stitch), O (long and short stitch), G (stem stitch)

Cornflower

Flower = I, AC, AF, AV or AW (2 strands, straight stitch), A (straight stitch)

Stem = AH (2 strands, heavy chain stitch)

Leaves = BD (split back stitch, long and short stitch)

Rabbit

Outline = AP (split back stitch)

Eye = AA (split back stitch, satin stitch), AQ (straight stitch)

Ears = AM or AP (long and short stitch), AN (straight stitch)

Head = AP (long and short stitch)

Nose = AN (satin stitch)

Front legs = AM (satin stitch), AP (split back stitch)

Back = AP (split back stitch, satin stitch)

Tummy = AQ (satin stitch)

Back legs = AP (satin stitch, split back stitch), AM (satin stitch)

Tail = AQ (Ghiordes knot)

Door

Door = AO (Cretan stitch variation)

Frame = AK (stem stitch)

Door knob = BM (beading)

Field flowers and grass

Grass = AH or BE (2 strands, straight stitch)

Pink anemone = L or M (2 strands, raised cross stitch), AA (2 strands, colonial knot)

Cream daisies = AE (2 strands, detached chain), V (2 strands, colonial knot)

Blue forget-me-nots = I (2 strands, granitos, 3 stitches), V (2 strands, colonial knot)

Tiny buds = I (2 strands, colonial knot)

Eyelets and charms = AD (running stitch, back stitch, overcast stitch)

Autumn Orange

BACK WALL

The orange tree was originally intended to be an apple tree, but with a strawberry bush on another wall I felt it would be all too red. I was fortunate enough to find a particular dye lot of Colour Streams Silken Strands 'Uluru' that reminded me of Valencia oranges.

THREADS & BEADS

Refer to the combined list of threads on page 11.

Au Papillon Fil d'Or Deluxe
B

Au Ver à Soie Antique Metallics
D

Au Ver à Soie, Soie d'Alger
G, I

Caron Soie Cristale stranded silk
L, M

Colour Streams Silken Strands
V

DMC stranded cotton
AA, AD, AE, AG, AH, AI, AJ

Gloriana Lorikeet stranded wool
AL, AM

YLI fine metallic
BK

Beads

Mill Hill seed beads
BN

Embroidery

See the liftout pattern for the orange basket templates.

Follow the general embroidery instructions on page 9. Refer to the close-up photograph and embroidery key for colour placement, and the needle chart on page 10 for the use of needles.

Order of work

ORANGE TREE

Trunk and branches

The roots, trunk and branches are embroidered in alternating rows of stem stitch and outline stitch with AL. Use one strand of yarn for the roots and the small branches and two strands for the trunk and the lower sections of the four larger branches.

Working stem stitch, begin at the tip of a root. As you reach the trunk join a second strand of yarn, matching the shading, and continue in stem stitch along the trunk. To return to one strand along the branch, slide one strand from the needle and secure on the back before you continue to the tip of the branch. Stitch the second row in a similar manner using outline stitch. To finish the row, tuck the last stitch under the stem stitch to achieve a smooth join (diag 17).

diag 17

Oranges

Stitching from the top of the fruit, cover an orange with closely worked long-armed cross stitch, using three strands of V. Gradually increase the width of the stitches for the upper half of the orange.

Smooth each stitch by placing your needle under the thread as you pull the stitch through so that the three strands lay side by side (diag 18).

diag 18

From the halfway point, gradually decrease the width of the stitches to achieve a smooth round shape. Work a tiny cross stitch at the base of the orange with two strands of AG.

> **HINT**
>
> *Long-armed cross stitch*
>
> I chose this stitch for the oranges because the crossing action and backward step gives a raised appearance, so I did not need to pad the fruit.

Leaves

Embroider the leaves in a similar manner to the rose leaves on page 14 using two strands of G, AI or AJ.

To add gold highlights or veins, bring one strand of D to the front at the edge of the leaf, slide your needle between two adjacent stitches and take it to the back at an angle under the centre line of anchoring stitches.

BASKET OF ORANGES

Refer to the step-by-step instructions for working Portuguese knotted stem stitch on page 94.

Using the pencil, trace the two basket templates onto appliqué paper. Fuse the paper onto the brown felt and cut out along the pencil lines, then remove the paper backing. Centre the smallest piece at the position for the basket and stab stitch in place with matching machine thread. Place the larger shape on top and work a stab stitch at each corner to ensure the basket is straight (*diag 19*).

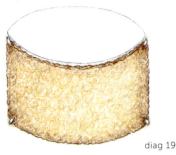

diag 19

Secure each side with small stab stitches. Using two strands of AM in the no. 5 crewel needle, cover the felt padding with woven filling stitch, working two rows for each weaving sequence.

Work the rim of the basket in Portuguese knotted stem stitch using the same thread. To keep the distinctive scroll of this stitch facing upwards, work the lower edge from (a) to (b) first. Return to (a) and work the upper edge of the rim to (b) (*diag 20*).

diag 20

Using AM, work five vertical straight stitches inside the rim and weave in the same pattern as before, but with just one strand (*diag 21*).

diag 21

Using two strands of AM, work a row of whipped chain stitch along the base of the basket. Stitch the handles in a similar manner using one strand of the same thread.

Fill the basket with orange seed beads (BN), stitched in place using two strands of AJ.

BEE

Refer to the step-by-step instructions for working trellis stitch on page 98.

Body

Using two strands of B, outline the body in small back stitches. Rotate the work so the base of the body is towards you. Change to the no. 26 tapestry needle and work six trellis stitches into six back stitches across the end of the body (*diag 22*).

diag 22

Continue to fill the body with trellis stitch, anchoring each row onto the back stitches. If necessary, increase a stitch at each end of a couple of rows to cover the wider part of the body. As the body becomes narrower, gradually decrease to one stitch.

Thorax and head

Work three small satin stitches across the upper end of the body for the thorax and work another two stitches over the top (*diag 23*).

diag 23

Using the same thread, work a colonial knot for the head.

Wings

Using BK, bring the thread to the front next to the thorax, just behind the head. Partially work a detached chain and, without anchoring the stitch, continue to embroider the wing in blanket stitch (*diag 24*).

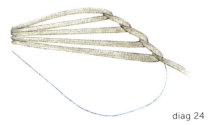

diag 24

Legs and Antennae

Using D, embroider three straight stitches for each leg and a straight stitch for each antenna.

FIELD FLOWERS AND GRASS

Refer to the step-by-step instructions for raised cross stitch on page 95.

Embroider the field flowers and grass across the lower edge of the panel in a similar manner to the front panel on page 16.

EYELETS AND CHARMS

Refer to the step-by-step instructions for working eyelets on page 86.

Using AD, work eyelets to attach the beehive charm on the right hand side of the orange tree and the rabbit charm on the left hand side. Stitch the owl charm in place among the branches using the clear nylon thread.

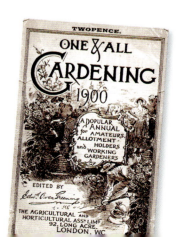

EMBROIDERY KEY

All embroidery is worked with one strand of thread unless otherwise specified.

Orange tree

Trunk and branches = AL (1 or 2 strands, outline stitch, stem stitch)

Oranges = V (3 strands, long-armed cross stitch), AG (2 strands, cross stitch)

Leaves = G, AI or AJ (2 strands, fly stitch), D (straight stitch)

Basket of oranges

Basket = AM
(2 strands, woven filling stitch)

Rim = AM (2 strands, Portuguese knotted stem stitch)

Filling = AM (woven filling stitch)

Base = AM
(2 strands, chain stitch, whipping)

Handles = AM
(chain stitch, whipping)

Oranges = AJ and BN
(2 strands, beading)

Bee

Body, thorax and head = B
(2 strands, back stitch, trellis stitch, satin stitch, colonial knot)

Wings = BK
(detached chain, blanket stitch)

Legs and antennae = D
(straight stitch)

Field flowers and grass

Grass = AH or BE
(2 strands, straight stitch)

Pink anemone = L or M
(2 strands, raised cross stitch),
AA (2 strands, colonial knot)

Cream daisies = AE
(2 strands, detached chain),
V (2 strands, colonial knot)

Blue forget-me-nots = I
(2 strands, granitos, 3 stitches),
V (2 strands, colonial knot)

Tiny buds = I
(2 strands, colonial knot)

Eyelets = AD (running stitch, back stitch, overcast stitch)

Spring Pea

PEA END WALL

The use of the pea plant harks back to traditional cottage gardens that were not just pretty, but practical as well, filled with food and herbs. The inspiration for the pea plant came from *A Book of Flowers, Fruits, Beasts, Birds, and Flies: Seventeenth-Century Patterns for Embroiderers* by Peter Stent.

THREADS & BEADS

Refer to the combined list of threads on page 11.

Au Papillon Fil d'Or deluxe
B

Au Ver à Soie Antique Metallics
D

Au Ver à Soie, Soie d'Alger
G, H, I

Caron Soie Cristale stranded silk
L, M, O, P, Q

Colour Streams Silken Strands
S, T, U, V

DMC no. 8 perlé cotton
X

DMC stranded cotton
Z, AA, AB, AD, AE, AH

Gumnut Yarns 'Stars' stranded silk
AR, AT, AU

Rajmahal stranded rayon
AX, AY

Threadworx stranded variegated cotton
BC

Weeks Dye Works stranded cotton
BE

YLI silk floss
BF, BH, BI

Beads & sequins

Mill Hill petite seed beads
BO, BP

Non-branded craft beads & sequins
BQ, BR

Embroidery

See the liftout pattern for the snail shell templates.

Follow the general embroidery instructions on page 9. Refer to the close-up photograph and embroidery key for colour placement, and the needle chart on page 10 for the use of needles.

Order of work

WINDOW

Appliqué and embroider the window following the instructions for the front wall on pages 13–14.

PEA PLANT

Refer to the step-by-step instructions for working Hungarian braided chain stitch on page 87, interlaced chain stitch on page 88 and ladder stitch on page 90.

Main stem

Stitching from the base to the tip, embroider the main stem in Hungarian braided chain stitch using two strands of O. Using B in the fine tapestry needle, whip around the inside chains only (*diag 25*).

diag 25

Stalks

Stitching from the base, work the pea stalks in coral stitch using two strands of AR, placing the knots close together. Work a row of outline stitch along the outer curve of each stalk with O. Changing to D, whip following the direction of the outline stitches (*diag 26*).

diag 26

Embroider a row of coral stitch for the stalks of each pea flower, using AR for the right hand flower and P for the left hand flower.

Tendrils

Stitch the large centre tendril in coral stitch using two strands of AR. Embroider the small tendrils in stem stitch with one strand of P, keeping the stitches short to follow the tight curves.

Left hand pea

The centre of the pea is embroidered in interlaced chain stitch. Using two strands of AR, begin at the top and work a row of large chain stitches along the centre to the tip of the pea. Lace each side of the chain stitches loosely, using two strands of Q in a tapestry needle and working each row from the top to the tip. Change to one strand of AY and couch the lacing thread at the outermost points to pull it slightly open (*diag 27*).

diag 27

Attach a tiny green sequin (BR) inside each chain with a colonial knot using two strands of AY.

Changing to two strands of P, outline the pea in whipped chain stitch, stitching each side from the top to the tip.

Right hand pea

Stitching from the top to the tip, work the right hand pea in ladder stitch with two strands of AR. Slightly increase the spacing of the stitches along the left hand side as you near the tip to swing the stitches around the curve.

Secure a length of X and bring it to the front at the centre top. Lay the perlé thread over the ladder stitch down the centre of the pea. Secure and bring three strands of O to the front at the same position. Work a coral knot over the laid thread, close to the emerging threads (*diag 28*).

diag 28

Work another six evenly spaced coral knots over the laid thread, allowing enough space between for six tiny sequins. Using the fine beading thread, attach six sequins (BR), each with a tiny bead (BP), between the coral knots (*diag 29*).

diag 29

Sepals

Outline each sepal with very small split back stitches using P. Fill the shape with horizontal satin stitches, working within the outline.

Starting in the middle of the upper section of the sepal, work long and short stitch towards one side, using O. Bring the thread to the front inside the shape and take the needle to the back just outside the outline, angling the needle back towards the sepal. Fan out the stitches to follow the direction of the shape (*diag 30*).

diag 30

Return to the halfway point and work long and short stitch across the remaining side in the same manner. Change to P and cover the lower section of the sepal in long and short stitch, bringing the needle to the front through the previous stitches and to the back outside the lower outline. Where required, work two rows of shorter stitches so they follow the curve of the sepal.

FLOWERS AND BUD

Bud

Outline the bud with very small split back stitches, using Z. Starting midway along the lower half of the petal, work long and

short stitch over the split back stitch outline. Angle the stitches towards the stalk end of the bud. As you near the side, gradually alter the direction of the stitches so they are parallel to the edge. Stitch the remaining half of the lower section in the same manner. Splitting the previous stitches, fill the upper section of the bud in long and short stitch in a similar manner.

Work three long straight stitches over the previous stitching using AX, and a few straight stitches using BI in the spaces between, for the highlights.

Flowers

Embroider the upper flower first. Using S, work split back stitch along the outer edge of the centre petal. Outline the two side petals in a similar manner using H, and the lower petal using Z. Changing to H, pad the two outer petals with satin stitch worked across each shape inside the outline.

Fill the centre petal with long and short stitch using S, covering the outline. Change to Z and cover the tiny petal at the base of the flower with satin stitch worked along the length of the petal (*diag 31*).

diag 31

Embroider the side petals in a similar manner to the centre petal, using H and angling the direction of the stitches towards the stalk.

Embroider the highlights on the centre petal in straight stitches using BH, and on the side petals using BF.

Embroider the lower flower in a similar manner.

Sepals

The sepals for the bud and flowers are all worked in the same manner using P.

Outline the sepal with very small split back stitches. Stitch three layers of satin stitch padding within this outline. Work the first layer across the shape a short distance inside the outline, followed by a second layer along the length of the shape. Stitch the top layer across the width, working just inside the outline (*diag 32*).

diag 32

Starting midway along the upper half of the sepal, work long and short stitch to one side, covering the outline and angling your stitches towards the stalk. Return to the centre and work across to the opposite side in the same manner. Cover the remaining half of the sepal, splitting the ends of the stitches in the previous row.

Leaf

Outline the leaf with small split back stitches using AR. Embroider the outer edge of the leaf in long and short stitch with the same thread, working each stitch from inside the shape and over the outline. Gradually change the angle of the stitches to indicate the direction of the veins.

HINT *Padded satin stitch*

When stitching several layers of satin stitch padding, each layer of stitches has to be in the opposite direction to the previous layer.

It is important that the top layer of padding is always worked in the opposite direction to the final layer of stitches.

Thread one strand each of O and G into separate needles and work the second row of long and short stitch, splitting the end of the stitches in the previous row and changing between the two threads. The greater the difference between the tones of green, the more staggered the boundary should be.

HINT
Multiple threads

I work a few stitches with one thread, leave a space or two, then work a few with the other tone. Always leave the spare thread on top of your work, so it will not get caught.

Leave a tiny space along the centre of the leaf for the vein. Stitching from the base towards the tip, work the centre vein in stem stitch using U. Embroider long straight stitches for the veins using the same thread. Change to D and work straight stitch highlights along the veins.

CATERPILLAR

Using three strands of Q in the no. 5 milliner's needle, work a 30-wrap bullion knot. Shape and couch the knot in place with a few stitches, using one strand of the same thread. Work a colonial knot for the head.

Changing to D, work a few tiny straight stitches for the legs.

SNAIL

Refer to the step-by-step instructions for working ladder stitch on page 90.

Shell

Outline the shell in split back stitch with BC.

Trace the shell templates onto appliqué paper. With the paper side uppermost, fuse the tracing to a small piece of brown wool felt and cut out along the marked lines. Remove the paper backing. Centre the smallest piece inside the shell outline and secure with stab stitches using matching machine sewing thread. Position and secure the larger piece over the top. Draw the spiral of the shell on the felt with the pencil (*diag 33*).

diag 33

Using two strands of BC, cover the lower section of the shell with ladder stitch. To accommodate the curve of the shell, alter the width of the ladder stitch and increase the spacing between the stitches along the lower edge to ensure all stitches are at a right angle to the outline (*diag 34*).

diag 34

Using the same thread, stitch a row of raised chain band along the centre of the ladder stitch.

Starting at the centre of the spiral, work short blanket stitches into the same hole at the top. As you near the completion of the first round, continue around the shape by gradually increasing the spacing of the stitches along the outer edge and working the inside edge closely against the first round of stitches to form a spiral (*diag 35*).

diag 35

Body and tail

Beginning near the shell, work straight stitch bars across the body at 2.5mm (1/16") intervals, using BC.

Change to the fine tapestry needle and pass the thread under the bars on the back of your work. Emerge at the lower edge, angling the needle from under the shell (*diag 36*).

diag 36

Work raised stem stitch into the bars, working each row from the shell to the head, pushing them close together.

Embroider the tail in a similar manner, stitching each row from the tip and tucking the last stitch under the shell. To achieve a nice point for the tail, start each row a needle width further out from the point (*diag 37*).

diag 37

To complete the shell, work outline stitch along the lower edge of the shell, and the purl edge of the spiralling upper section with D.

Antennae and eyes

Work a long straight stitch for each antenna using D. Stitch a bead (BO) in place with fine beading thread at the top of each for the eyes.

LADYBIRD

Body

Outline the body with split back stitch using AT. Pad the body with three layers of satin stitch within the outline, using the same thread. Each layer of stitches is perpendicular to the previous.

Covering the outline, embroider the final layer of satin stitch along the length of the body, beginning at the centre and stitching one side at a time. Bring the needle to the front at an angle from under the outline on one side and take it to the back at an angle on the other, so that the stitches hug the split back stitch.

Changing to AA, scatter nine seed stitches over the body for the spots. Take care not to pull too tightly and disturb the underlying satin stitches.

Head

Outline the head in split back stitch with AA. Embroider four or five satin stitches across the head, covering the outline. Work a small straight stitch for each antenna.

Legs

Work two front legs at the junction of the head and body, and two legs evenly spaced along each side of the body using AA. Stitch three short straight stitches for each leg to achieve the correct shape (*diag 38*).

diag 38

FIELD FLOWERS AND GRASS

Refer to the step-by-step instructions for raised cross stitch on page 95.

Embroider the field flowers and grass along the lower edge of the panel following the instructions on page 16.

Wheat

Using two strands of T, work the wheat in feather stitch.

Dill weed

To embroider the dill weed, work the stems in stem stitch and fly stitch with BE. Embroider the flower head with five to seven pistil stitches of varying lengths, fanning out from the top of the stem.

EYELETS, CHARMS AND BEADS

Refer to the step-by-step instructions for working eyelets on page 86.

Using AD, work an eyelet and attach the ladybird charm to the left of the pea plant. Stitch the lizard charm in place using the fine beading thread, and the three blue flower beads (BQ) using matching machine sewing thread.

EMBROIDERY KEY

All embroidery is worked using one strand of thread unless otherwise specified.

Window

Panes = AB (2 strands, straight stitch), BB (2 strands, lacing)

Frame = AU
(Portuguese border stitch)

Mullion = AU
(2 strands, chain stitch, whipping)

Pea

Stems, stalks and tendrils

Main stem = O (2 strands, Hungarian braided chain stitch), B (whipping)

Pea stalks = AR (2 strands, coral stitch), O (outline stitch), D (whipping)

Flower stalks = P or AR
(2 strands, coral stitch)

Tendrils = AR (2 strands, coral stitch), P (stem stitch)

Pea pods

Left hand pea = Q and AR
(2 strands, interlaced chain stitch), AY (couching), AY and BR (2 strands, colonial knot), P (2 strands, chain stitch, whipping)

Right hand pea = AR (2 strands, ladder stitch), X and O (3 strands, corded coral stitch), BR and BP (attaching sequins)

Sepals = P (split back stitch, satin stitch), O and P (long and short stitch)

Flowers and bud

Bud = Z (split back stitch, long and short stitch), AX or BI (straight stitch)

Flowers = H, S and Z (split back stitch, long and short stitch), BH or BF (straight stitch)

Sepals = P (split back stitch, satin stitch, long and short stitch)

Leaf = AR (split back stitch, long and short stitch), O and G (long and short stitch), U (stem stitch, straight stitch), D (straight stitch)

Caterpillar

Body = Q (3 strands, bullion knot, 30 wraps, 1 strand, couching)

Head = Q (3 strands, colonial knot)

Legs = D (straight stitch)

Snail

Shell, lower section = BC (split back stitch, 2 strands, ladder stitch, raised chain band), D (outline stitch)

Shell, upper section = BC (2 strands, blanket stitch), D (outline stitch)

Body and tail = BC (raised stem band)

Antennae and eyes = D (straight stitch), BO (beading)

Ladybird

Body = AT (split back stitch, padded satin stitch), AA (seed stitch)

Head = AA
(split back stitch, satin stitch)

Antennae and legs = AA
(straight stitch)

Field flowers and grass

Grass = AH or BE
(2 strands, straight stitch)

Pink anemone = L or M (2 strands, raised cross stitch), AA (2 strands, colonial knot)

Cream daisies = AE
(2 strands, detached chain), V (2 strands, colonial knot)

Blue forget-me-nots = I
(2 strands, granitos, 3 stitches), V (2 strands, colonial knot)

Tiny buds = I (2 strands, colonial knot)

Wheat = T (2 strands, feather stitch)

Dill weed = BE
(stem stitch, fly stitch, pistil stitch)

Eyelets = AD (running stitch, back stitch, overcast stitch)

Summer Strawberry

STRAWBERRY END WALL

This design was adapted from a panel on a stumpwork box I saw on an episode of Antiques Roadshow — always worth recording. They often show excellent close-up shots of textiles, enamels and more. You can hit the pause button and sketch.

THREADS & BEADS

Refer to the combined list of threads on page 11.

Au Papillon Fil d'Or deluxe
A, B

Au Ver à Soie Antique Metallics
C, D

Au Ver à Soie, Soie d'Alger stranded silk
G, I, K

Caron Soie Cristale stranded silk
M, N, O

Caron Wildflowers perlé cotton
R

Colour Streams Silken Strands
T, U, V

DMC no. 4 soft cotton
Y

DMC stranded cotton
AA, AE, AH

Gumnut Yarns 'Stars' stranded silk
AR, AS

Rajmahal stranded rayon
AY

The Gentle Art Sampler Threads
BA

Weeks Dye Works stranded cotton
BE

Beads

Maria George Delica beads
BL

Non-branded craft beads
BQ

Embroidery

See the liftout pattern for the strawberry templates.

Follow the general embroidery instructions on page 9. Refer to the close-up photograph and embroidery key for colour placement, and the needle chart on page 10 for the use of needles.

Order of work

STRAWBERRY BUSH

Refer to the step-by-step instructions for working the knotted pearl stitch on page 89, needlewoven picots on page 91 and Rococo stitch variation on page 95.

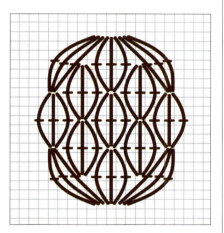

Main stem

Embroider the stem in knotted pearl stitch with three strands of AS. Begin at the top of the stem and increase the width of the stitches after the upper right hand leaf.

Strawberries

Using the pencil, trace each strawberry template twice onto appliqué paper. Fuse the paper onto the red wool felt and cut out along the pencil lines. Peel away the backing paper.

Centre a small piece at the position for one strawberry and stab stitch in place with matching thread. With the adhesive side uppermost, place the larger piece on top and attach as before. Repeat for the remaining strawberry.

Cut two 2.5cm (1") squares of 14-count waste canvas. Tack a piece in place over each padded strawberry, aligning the grain down the length of the strawberry.

Using BA and beginning at the centre top of the berry, work a row of Rococo stitch variation across the upper edge of the padded shape, keeping the couching stitches aligned. To achieve a nice smooth, rounded shape, work the outermost stitches a little loosely to elongate each lozenge shape on one side *(diag 39)*.

diag 39

Embroider the second row in a similar manner, interlocking the stitches into the first row. Continue to work rows to fill the shape, adjusting the stitches at the sides to achieve a smooth edge.

Carefully withdraw the canvas threads with the eye of a needle.

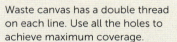

HINT

Rococo stitch variation

Waste canvas has a double thread on each line. Use all the holes to achieve maximum coverage.

I recommend you practise this stitch first without padding, then with padding to really understand how to adapt the stitch to the shape.

If you do not pack the stitches close enough together, the red felt will show through. Positioning the top layer of padding with the adhesive side up helps lessen this, as well as preventing the fluff of the felt being dragged through the canvas.

To embroider the seeds, stitch French knots scattered across each berry using two strands of A. Take care not to pull the stitches too tight, so the knots sit on top of the previous stitching.

Using two strands of O, work three needlewoven picots at the top of each berry for the sepals.

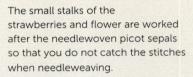

HINT
Stalks and sepals

The small stalks of the strawberries and flower are worked after the needlewoven picot sepals so that you do not catch the stitches when needleweaving.

Strawberry and flower stalks

Working from the main stem, embroider the stalk for the lower strawberry in chain stitch using two strands of AS. Slide the needle under the picots as you near the top of the berry. Changing to the fine tapestry needle and one strand of B, whip the row of chain stitch. Embroider the stem for the flower in the same manner. Stitch the stem for the unripe berry in a similar manner using two strands of AS for the whipping.

Unripe berry

Working from the edge of the berry towards the centre, fill the unripe berry with closely packed colonial knots using R. Use each section of the thread to create patches of colour.

Changing to two strands of O, stitch a large detached chain for each sepal. Using B, add a long straight stitch over each anchoring stitch for highlights (*diag 40*).

diag 40

Strawberry flower

Outline the petals in split back stitch using K, stitching a single row between the petals and around the flower centre (*diag 41*).

diag 41

Work two layers of satin stitch padding, ensuring the uppermost layer is worked across the width of the petals. Embroider satin stitch over the padding, bringing the thread to the front on the outer edge of the petal and taking the needle to the back over the outline on the inner edge. If your stitches become too crowded, work some 3/4 length stitches.

Changing to AR, work a straight stitch to mark the division between each petal. Embroider three straight stitches of differing lengths over each petal using AY. Fill the centre with colonial knots using two strands of T.

Stitch five small sepals between the petals using two strands of O, working three fishbone stitches for each.

Leaves

Outline each leaf with small split back stitches using AR. Embroider the outer edge of the three lower leaves in long and short stitch using the same thread and working each stitch from inside the shape and over the outline. Gradually change the angle of the stitches to follow the direction of the veins.

Thread one strand each of G and O into separate needles and work the second row of long and short stitch in a similar manner to the pea leaf on pages 24–25. Leave a narrow space down the middle of the leaf for the vein. Stitching from the base towards the tip of the leaf, work the centre vein in stem stitch using U. Embroider long straight stitches for the veins with the same thread. Change to D and work straight stitch highlights along the veins. Stitch the uppermost leaf in a similar manner, omitting the centre vein.

CATERPILLAR

The body is padded with two lengths of soft cotton (Y), laid side by side. Leaving 1cm (3/8") tails of soft cotton on the back, work two long parallel stitches within the outline, ensuring they are loose enough to follow the shape (*diag 42*).

diag 42

Fold the thread tails under the caterpillar on the wrong side and whip stitch in place with U. Using the same thread, embroider straight stitch bars across the padding, spacing the stitches 3mm (1/8") apart. Change to the fine tapestry needle and, starting on the underside of the caterpillar, work raised stem stitch. Stop and start each row on the marked outline to

create a rounded head and tail. Once all the bars are filled, couch across the caterpillar with one strand of O. Angle the stitches under the body and pull firmly to create little fat segments.

Embroider the legs with tiny pairs of straight stitches using C, and work two longer straight stitches into the same hole at the top for each horn (diag 43).

diag 43

Attach two beads (BL) for the eyes with the fine beading thread. Place a stitch over the thread between the beads to pull them into place (diag 44).

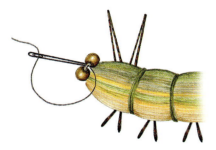

diag 44

FIELD FLOWERS AND GRASS

Refer to the step-by-step instructions for raised cross stitch on page 95.

Embroider the field flowers and grass along the lower edge of the panel following the instructions on page 16, using M or N for the anemones. Stitch the wheat and dill weed following the instructions on page 26.

CHARMS AND BEADS

Using the fine beading thread, stitch the three small bee charms in place around the strawberry plant and the beehive button next to stem. Attach three blue flower beads (BQ) above the caterpillar using matching thread.

EMBROIDERY KEY

All embroidery is worked using one strand of thread unless otherwise specified.

Strawberry bush

Main stem = AS
(3 strands, knotted pearl stitch)

Stawberries = BA
(2 strands, Rococo stitch variation)

Seeds = A (2 strands, French knot)

Sepals = O
(2 strands, needlewoven picot)

Strawberry and flower stalks = AS
(2 strands, chain stitch, whipping),
B (whipping)

Unripe strawberry = R (colonial knot)

Sepals = O (2 strands, detached chain),
B (straight stitch)

Flower = K (split back stitch, padded satin stitch), AR and AY (straight stitch), T (2 strands, colonial knot), O (2 strands, fishbone stitch)

Leaves = AR (split back stitch, long and short stitch), G and O (long and short stitch), U (stem stitch, straight stitch), D (straight stitch)

Caterpillar

Body = Y (straight stitch),
U (overcast stitch, raised stem stitch),
O (couching)

Legs and horns = C (straight stitch)

Eyes = BL (beading)

Field flowers and grass

Grass = AH or BE
(2 strands, straight stitch)

Pink anemone = M or N
(2 strands, raised cross stitch),
AA (2 strands, colonial knot)

Cream daisies = AE
(2 strands, detached chain),
V (2 strands, colonial knot)

Blue forget-me-nots = I
(2 strands, granitos, 3 stitches),
V (2 strands, colonial knot)

Tiny buds = I (2 strands, colonial knot)

Wheat = T (2 strands, feather stitch)

Dill weed = BE (stem stitch, fly stitch, pistil stitch)

ROOF

Cut the skein of W in half and use one length to thread under each row of satin stitch blocks.

EDGING AND CLOSURES

The edges and loops are embroidered as the roof is constructed.

EMBROIDERY KEY

All embroidery is worked using one strand of thread.

Tiles = W and BJ
(threaded satin stitch honeycomb)

Edging = W (Armenian edging stitch)

Chimney closures = W
(up and down blanket stitch loop)

BASE

O riginally the base was plain and the button feet just stitched on the outside. I did not like seeing the linen shank, so my husband drilled holes in the cardboard for the button shanks to sit in.

THREADS

Refer to the combined list of threads on page 11.

Au Ver à Soie Antique Metallics
D

Au Ver à Soie, Soie d'Alger
I

Caron Soie Cristale stranded silk
M, N, O

Colour Streams Silken Strands
T

DMC stranded cotton
AA, AE

Gumnut 'Stars' stranded silk
AR

T he use of the variegated yarn for the roof was a lucky accident. I was planning to use a different thread, but I ran out of it in January, when all the wholesalers in Australia close for a few weeks. I decided to try the variegated yarn instead. It was a much better choice since it gives greater depth to the embroidery and the blocks look even more tile-like.

THREADS

Refer to the combined list of threads on page 11.

DMC no. 5 perlé cotton
W

YLI Multi's Embellishment Yarn
BJ

Embroidery

See page 9 for the general embroidery instructions.

Order of work

TILES

Refer to the step-by-step instructions for working the threaded satin stitch honeycomb on page 97.

Embroider each roof piece in threaded satin stitch honeycomb referring to diagram 46, using BJ for the satin stitch blocks and W for the threading.

Work eighteen horizontal rows of fifteen satin stitch blocks on each roof section. Each satin stitch block is worked over four fabric threads, except the uppermost row of the back roof panel. This row of stitches is worked over three fabric threads, to accommodate the opening edge *(diag 45)*.

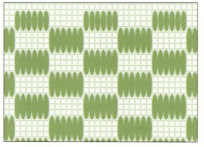

diag 45

Embroidery

See page 9 for the general embroidery instructions.

Order of work

OVAL

Refer to the step-by-step instructions for working the Hungarian braided chain stitch on page 87.

Stitch the upper and lower sections of the oval in Hungarian braided chain stitch with two strands of O. Work a row of stem stitch on each side of the Hungarian braided chain stitch using D.

LETTERING

Using two strands of O, embroider the lettering in back stitch.

FLOWERS

Refer to the step-by-step instructions for raised cross stitch on page 95 and rosette stitch on page 96.

Pink anemones

Embroider the three anemones at each end of the design in raised cross stitch with two strands of M or N. Change to two strands of AA and work a colonial knot at the centre of each flower.

Roses

Using two strands of N, work a rosette stitch for each of the two smaller roses at each end, adding a colonial knot at the centre.

Forget-me-nots

Stitch a colonial knot at the marked position for the centre of each forget-me-not using two strands of T.

Embroider colonial knot petals around each flower centre using two strands of AE for the cream flowers and one strand of I for the blue. To achieve even spacing of the petals, place the first knot directly below the centre and the following two side by side above the centre knot *(diag 46)*.

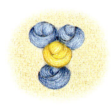

diag 46

To complete the flower, place a knot in the remaining space on each side of the centre for petals 4 and 5.

Foliage

Using AR, stitch detached chains for the leaves. Add smaller leaves using D in the same manner. Embroider the stems in straight stitch with AR, placing a tiny couching stitch over the longer stitches to achieve a curve.

EYELETS

Refer to the step-by-step instructions for working eyelets on page 86.

Using AD, embroider an eyelet at the marked positions at each corner for attaching the covered button feet after the base is constructed.

EMBROIDERY KEY

All embroidery is worked using one strand of thread unless otherwise specified.

Oval = O (2 strands, Hungarian braided chain stitch), D (stem stitch)

Lettering = O (2 strands, back stitch)

Flowers

Anemones = M or N (2 strands, raised cross stitch), AA (2 strands, colonial knot)

Roses = N (2 strands, rosette stitch, colonial knot)

Forget-me-nots = T (2 strands, colonial knot), AE (2 strands) or I (colonial knot)

Foliage

Leaves = D or AR (detached chain)

Stems = AR (straight stitch, couching)

Eyelets = AD (running stitch, back stitch, overcast stitch)

Construction

Boxes are always constructed from the outside in, beginning with the outer walls and base, followed by the lining and its base. Once the main box is complete, you construct the walls and base of the liftout tray, followed by the lining of the liftout tray. I adopted Jackie Woolsey's method of attaching the risers to each wall lining before stitching the lining walls together. The shaded areas in the following diagrams indicate the right side of the fabric.

Cutting out

Conversions from metric to imperial measurements have been provided as accurately as possible. To achieve a good result, however, it is strongly recommended that you work from the metric measurements when measuring and cutting.

MOUNTBOARD

Refer to the instructions for marking and cutting mountboard on page 9.

Do not cut out all the mountboard at once. Cut out and construct one section of the box at a time, before moving on to the next section. This makes it easy to trim pieces as necessary to ensure a perfect fit. Mark the grain of the card at one corner and ensure each piece is cut correctly along the grain *(diag 1)*.

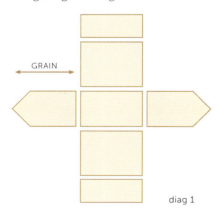

GRAIN

diag 1

LINING FABRIC

If you are using a striped or checked fabric for the lining, you will need to match the stripes each time you cut a piece. Have the sections already finished in front of you.

Outer box

2mm (^{1}/$_8$") mountboard

Front and back walls: cut two, each 11.5cm x 15.4cm wide (4 ^{1}/$_2$" x 6 ^{1}/$_{16}$")

End walls: cut two, each 9cm x 16cm wide (3 ^{9}/$_{16}$" x 6 ^{5}/$_{16}$")

Base: cut one, 9cm x 15.4cm wide (3 ^{9}/$_{13}$" x 6 ^{1}/$_{16}$")

Back roof: cut one, 6.4cm x 16cm wide (2 ^{9}/$_{13}$" x 6 ^{5}/$_{16}$")

Front roof: cut one, 6.5cm x 16cm wide (2 ^{9}/$_{16}$" x 6 ^{5}/$_{16}$")

Trimming the base

The base of the outer box is set into the four walls. The best way to achieve an accurate fit is to mark the rectangle measuring 9cm x 15.4cm wide (3 ^{9}/$_{16}$" x 6 ^{1}/$_{16}$"), matching the width of the wall and end wall pieces.

Hold two scrap pieces of mountboard together and mark their thickness at one end of the base piece *(diag 2)*.

diag 2

Using the set square, draw a new line at the marked position before trimming the base piece to size.

Shaping the gable ends

Measure and mark the centre of one short edge of an end wall piece for the top of the gable. Measure and mark 11.5cm (4 ^{1}/$_2$") along each side from

each lower corner. Rule a line from the marked point on each side to the centre mark *(diag 3)*.

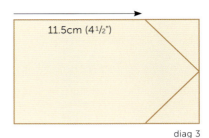

11.5cm (4^1/$_2$")

diag 3

Recut along the marked lines. Repeat for the second end wall piece.

White felt

Using the mountboard pieces as templates, cut the felt padding pieces slightly larger than the corresponding mountboard pieces.

Front and back walls: cut two

End walls: cut two, after the gables are cut to shape

Base: cut one, after the base is trimmed to size.

Back roof: cut one

Front roof: cut one

Box lining

Construct and check the measurements of the outer box before cutting the panels for the lining.

2mm (^{1}/$_8$") mountboard

Front and back walls: cut two, each 11cm x 15cm wide (4 ^{5}/$_{16}$" x 5 ^{7}/$_8$")

End walls: cut two, each 15.5cm x 8.5cm wide (6 ^{1}/$_8$" x 3 ^{3}/$_8$")

Base: cut one, 14.6cm x 8.5cm wide (5 ^{3}/$_4$" x 3 ^{5}/$_{16}$")

Back roof lining: cut one 6cm x 14.7cm wide (2 ^{3}/$_8$" x 5 ^{13}/$_{16}$")

Front roof lining: cut one 5.7cm x 14.7cm wide (2 ^{1}/$_4$" x 5 ^{13}/$_{16}$")

Long risers: cut two, each 5.5cm x 14.6cm wide (2 ^{1}/$_8$" x 5 ^{3}/$_4$")

Short risers: cut two, each 5.5cm x 8.1cm wide (2 ^{1}/$_8$" x 3 ^{3}/$_{16}$")

Shaping the gable ends

Cut the end wall gables to shape in a similar manner to the outer walls, measuring 11.3 cm (4 ^{7}/$_{16}$") from the lower corners.

White felt

Using the mountboard piece as a template, cut the felt padding piece slightly larger than the corresponding mountboard piece.

Base: cut one

Pale butter and fern green print cotton

Match the fabric print on each piece if necessary.

Front and back walls: cut two, each 16cm x 20cm wide (6⁵/₁₆" x 7⁷/₈")

End walls: cut two, each 20.5cm x 13.5cm wide (8¹/₁₆" x 5⁵/₁₆") – (Trim the diagonal gables using the mountboard piece as a template and leaving 2.5cm (1") seam allowances)

Base: cut one, 19.5cm x 13.5cm wide (7³/₄" x 5⁵/₁₆")

Long risers: cut two, each 10.5cm x 19.5cm wide (4¹/₈" x 7¹/₂")

Short risers: cut two, each 10.5cm x 13cm wide (4¹/₈" x 5¹/₈")

Back roof lining: cut one 11cm x 19.6cm wide (4⁵/₁₆" x 7³/₄")

Front roof lining: cut one 10.5cm x 19.6cm wide (4¹/₈" x 7³/₄")

Covered elastic bands: cut one 24cm x 3cm wide (9¹/₂" x 1³/₁₆")

Liftout tray

Construct the lined box and check the measurements before cutting the pieces for the outer tray.

2mm (¹/₈") mountboard

Outer Tray

Long walls: cut two, each 4.5cm x 14.5cm wide (1³/₄" x 5¹¹/₁₆")

Short walls: cut two, each 8cm x 4.5cm wide (3³/₁₆" x 1³/₄")

Base: cut one, 8cm x 14.1cm wide (3³/₁₆" x 5⁹/₁₆")

Inner Tray

Construct the outer tray and check the measurements before cutting the pieces for the inner tray. Label each piece with pencil as you cut.

Long walls: cut two, each 4.2cm x 14cm wide (1⁵/₈" x 5¹/₂")

Short walls: cut two, each 7.5cm x 4.2cm wide (2¹⁵/₁₆" x 1⁵/₈")

Thimble holder base (A): cut one 3.7cm x 3.8cm wide (1⁷/₁₆" x 1¹/₂")

Emery block base (B): cut one 3.7cm x 2.6cm wide (1⁷/₁₆" x 1")

Tape measure base (C): cut one 3.5cm x 6.8cm wide (1³/₈" x 2¹¹/₁₆")

Spool holder base (D): cut one 7.5cm x 6.2cm wide (2¹⁵/₁₆" x 2⁷/₁₆")

1.5mm (¹/₁₆") mountboard

Construct the inner tray walls and check the measurements before cutting the pieces for the dividers.

Dividers:

(D1) Cut one, 3.7cm x 4.2cm wide (1⁷/₁₆" x 1⁵/₈")

(D2) Cut one, 6.8cm x 4.2cm wide (2¹¹/₁₆" x 1⁵/₈")

(D3) Cut one, 7.5cm x 4.2cm wide (2¹⁵/₁₆" x 1⁵/₈")

Fusible interfacing

Cut the fusible interfacing to the same measurements as the 1.5mm (¹/₁₆") mountboard.

White felt

Using the mountboard pieces as templates, cut each felt padding piece slightly larger than the corresponding mountboard piece.

Thimble holder base (A): cut one

Emery block base (B): cut one

Tape measure base (C): cut one

Spool holder base (D): cut one

Pale butter and fern green print cotton

Match the fabric print on each piece if necessary.

Outer Tray

Long walls: cut two, each 9.5cm x 19.5cm wide (3³/₄" x 7¹¹/₁₆")

Short walls: cut two, each 9.5cm x 13cm wide (3³/₄" x 5⁵/₁₆")

Base: cut one, 13cm x 19cm wide (3³/₄" x 7⁵/₈")

Inner Tray

Long walls: cut two, each 9.2cm x 19cm wide (3⁵/₈" x 7¹/₂")

Short walls: cut two, each 9.5cm x 12.5cm wide (3³/₄" x 4¹⁵/₁₆")

Thimble holder base (A): cut one 8.7cm x 8.8cm wide (3⁷/₁₆" x 3¹/₂")

Emery block base (B): cut one 8.7cm x 7.6cm wide (3⁷/₁₆" x 3")

Tape measure base (C): cut one 8.5cm x 11.8cm wide (3⁵/₁₆" x 4⁵/₈")

Spool holder base (D): cut one 12.5cm x 11.2cm wide (4¹⁵/₁₆" x 4³/₈")

Dividers

(D1) Cut one, 10.5cm x 5.7cm wide (4¹/₈" x 2¹/₄")

(D2) Cut one, 10.5cm x 8.8cm wide (4¹/₈" x 3¹/₂")

(D3) Cut one, 10.5cm x 9.5cm wide (4¹/₈" x 3³/₄")

Cutting layouts

2mm (⅛") mountboard

Outer box

1. Front and back wall
2. End wall
3. Base
4. Back roof
5. Front roof

Box lining

6. Front and back wall
7. End wall
8. Base
9. Back roof
10. Front roof
11. Long risers
12. Short risers

Outer tray

13. Long wall
14. Short wall
15. Base

Inner tray

16. Long walls
17. Short walls
18. Thimble holder base (A)
19. Emery block base (B)
20. Tape measure base (C)
21. Spool holder base (D)

1.5mm (1/16") mountboard

Inner tray

22. Divider (D1)
23. Divider (D2)
24. Divider (D3)

Fusible interfacing

Inner tray

25. Divider (D1)
26. Divider (D2)
27. Divider (D3)

Pale butter and fern green print cotton

Box lining

28. Front and back walls
29. End walls
30. Base
31. Long risers
32. Short risers
33. Back roof
34. Front roof
35. Covered elastic bands

Outer tray

36. Long walls
37. Short walls
38. Base

Inner tray

39. Long walls
40. Short walls
41. Thimble holder base (A)
42. Emery block base (B)
43. Tape measure base (C)
44. Spool holder base (D)
45. Divider (D1)
46. Divider (D2)
47. Divider (D3)

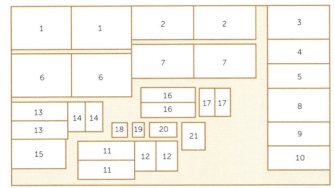

2mm (⅛") MOUNTBOARD – 56cm x 82cm wide (22" x 33")

1.5mm (1/16")
MOUNTBOARD
10cm (4") square

INTERFACING
5cm x 10cm wide
(2" x 4")

PALE BUTTER AND FERN GREEN PRINT COTTON
50cm x 115cm wide (20" x 46")

COMPLETED OUTER BOX

Order of work

House box

Refer to the step-by-step instructions for lacing and mitring corners over mountboard on page 88.

Every fabric piece is laced over mountboard and every fabric corner is mitred and handstitched to reduce the bulk of fabric, as well as ensure very neat corners where they are exposed.

1. Preparing the embroidered panels

To block the embroidered panels, place face down on the ironing board. Gently pulling the fabric taut and the grain straight, place pins on opposite edges at the midpoints of the fabric piece, angling them outwards. Continue to pin on opposite sides, keeping the grain straight and the fabric taut. Repeat for the remaining two sides. Steam with an iron, only pressing the fabric where the hoop has been. Once dry, remove the calico strips. Cut out the base and wall pieces along the marked cutting lines.

Cut out the roof pieces, leaving a 3cm (1³⁄₁₆") seam allowance on all four sides. Set aside until the walls and lining are complete.

2. Making the wall panels

Apply a tiny amount of glue to each corner of a wall mountboard piece using a small paintbrush. Position the felt padding over the mountboard and press lightly at the corners to secure. Leave to dry. Repeat for the remaining wall mountboard pieces and felt panels. Trim the felt flush with the mountboard edge, using scissors held hard against the board.

Centre an embroidered panel over the padded side of a corresponding mountboard piece and lace in place following the step-by-step instructions. It is a good idea to leave in the tacked outline to use as a guide until lacing is complete. Lace the remaining three wall pieces in the same manner.

3. Making the base and attaching the covered button feet

Drill a 5.5mm (¼") hole at each corner of the mountboard base 8mm (⁵⁄₁₆") from each corner *(diag 4)*.

diag 4

To achieve a neat hole and prevent the mountboard bending and softening, start with a small drill bit and work up to the 5.5mm (¼") drill bit.

Glue the felt padding to the base in the same manner as the walls. Working from the felt side, use the dressmaker's awl to pierce a hole through the felt at each corner.

Ensuring the embroidered eyelets are aligned with the holes in the mountboard, lace the embroidered base panel over the mountboard in the same manner as the walls.

Cover the buttons following the manufacturer's instructions. Push the shank of one button through a hole and secure to the seam allowance of the base fabric on the wrong side. Repeat for the remaining three buttons.

4. Constructing the outer walls

Pin one end wall to the inside edge of one long wall so that the walls are at right angles. Using the curved needle and matching machine sewing thread, ladder stitch the walls together from the outside *(diag 5)*.

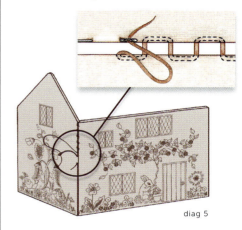

diag 5

Stitch the remaining end wall to the opposite end of the long wall piece in the same manner. Attach the remaining long wall to the opposite side as before, ensuring the edges of the end walls are aligned with the back edges of the long wall.

5. Attaching the base

Push the base into position inside the walls. Pin and ladder stitch the walls to the base *(diag 6)*.

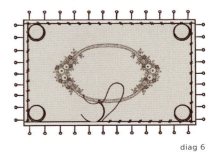

diag 6

HINTS

Joining laced mountboard panels

To achieve sturdy and smooth joins, secure the thread in the seam allowance 1.5cm (⁵⁄₈") from the upper corner (a). Ladder stitch up to the corner (b), then down to the lower corner (c) and back 1.5cm (⁵⁄₈") to (d).

Work a couple of back stitches to secure. Slide the needle between the layers and emerge a short distance away. Pull the thread taut and cut. The tail will spring back into the padding.

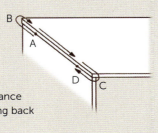

6. Preparing the lining pieces

Attach the felt padding to the base mountboard piece and trim. Lace and mitre the lining fabric pieces over the corresponding pieces of mountboard, including the risers, ensuring the fabric print is aligned on each piece.

7. Constructing the lining

With right sides facing up, position one long riser over one long wall piece, leaving a 2mm (1/8") space along the sides and base (diag 7).

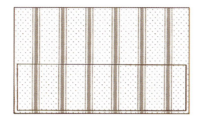

diag 7

Pin and ladder stitch in place along the ends and lower edge, leaving the upper edge of the riser free. Repeat for the remaining long riser. Attach the two short risers to the lower edge of each end wall in the same manner.

With the laced sides facing out, join the lining walls at right angles in a similar manner to the outer box, stitching from the laced side of each piece (diag 8).

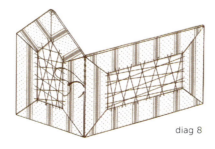

diag 8

Push the base of the lining into position against the lower edges of the risers. Pin and ladder stitch the walls to the base on the wrong side.

Making and attaching the cord stays

Cut four 90cm (35 1/2") lengths of BG. Knot the threads together and make a twisted cord. Measure 6cm (2 3/8") from the folded end and wrap the cord tightly using one strand of the same

thread. Take a few stitches through the wraps to secure (diag 9).

diag 9

Measure and wrap again 1cm (3/8") from the first wrapping. Cut the cord midway between the two wrapped points (diag 10).

diag 10

Measure and wrap in the same manner to form four 6cm (2 3/8") cords for the stays.

Measure 2.5cm (1") from the lower edge of the gable. Securely stitch the end of one cord stay in the seam allowance of the lining (diag 11).

diag 11

Stitch the remaining three stays in place in the same manner.

8. Inserting the box lining

Slide the box lining inside the outer box. Ladder stitch together along the tops of the front and back walls and the gables, making sure the stays are left free.

Roof

Refer to the step-by-step instructions for working Armenian edging stitch on page 83 and up and down blanket stitch loop on page 99.

9. Preparing the roof panels

Apply a tiny amount of glue at each corner of the mountboard and glue the felt in place. When dry, trim the felt flush with the board.

Lace each embroidered panel over the corresponding mountboard piece, mitring all four corners with matching machine sewing thread. These mitres will show on the outer edge of each corner, so pay particular attention to your stitching.

EDGING

Embroider Armenian edging stitch with one strand of W around the entire edge of the front roof panel. Starting along one short end, repeat for the back roof panel, omitting the upper opening edge.

CLOSURE

Using doubled, waxed brown machine sewing thread, attach a green nephrite cylinder bead with a 4mm (3/16") round brown bead for each chimney on the back roof ridge line. Each one is positioned four satin stitch blocks in from the short edge (diag 12).

diag 12

Secure a length of W and emerge two satin stitch blocks from the short edge. Work a triple loop over three satin stitch blocks, making sure the loop fits very snug over the bead chimney (*diag 13*).

diag 13

Work up and down blanket stitch over the triple loop, pushing the stitches closely together to form a firm loop. Repeat for the second loop.

10. Constructing the roof linings

Preparing the covered elastic bands

Fold the strip in half along the length with right sides together and matching raw edges. Machine stitch 9mm ($^5/_{16}$") from the folded edge. Turn the strip to the right side using a loop turner.

Thread a $^1/_4$-inch press bar through the casing and press the seam flat in the middle of the casing. Remove the bar and press again. Edge stitch along each side of the strip.

Mark the midpoint and thread the elastic into the casing. Secure the elastic at one end of the casing with a few hand stitches.

Attaching the covered elastic band

Pin a piece of lining fabric over the corresponding piece of mountboard for the roof lining. Pin the secured end of the band in position on the lining, within the seam allowance (*diag 14*).

SEAM ALLOWANCE

diag 14

Stretch the elastic inside the casing to fit snugly over each of your tools and pin in place, inserting a pin between tools if desired. Continue laying the casing across the lining piece until you reach the opposite seam allowance.

At this point, handstitch the elastic to the casing as before, then work a second row of handstitching 1cm ($^3/_8$") away.

Cut the elastic casing in half between the rows of handstitching (*diag 15*).

diag 15

Remove the lining fabric with the pinned elastic casing from the mountboard. Machine stitch at each pin mark, as well as across the ends of the fabric casing in the seam allowance of the lining (*diag 16*).

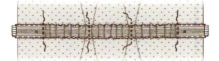

diag 16

Pull the machine threads to the wrong side of the lining fabric, thread the tails into a needle and secure. Stitch a tiny button securely in place at each end of the covered band. Construct the remaining roof lining fabric piece in the same manner.

Lace and mitre each piece of lining fabric over the corresponding mountboard piece.

11. Attaching the roof linings

Secure the end of a twisted cord stay at the midpoint in the seam allowance at each short end of one lining piece. The stays should measure 5.5cm (2 $^1/_8$") (*diag 17*).

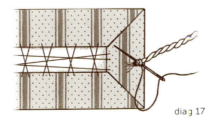

diag 17

Repeat for the remaining lining and cord stays.

Pin each roof lining panel to the wrong side of the corresponding roof section, leaving a 4mm ($^3/_{16}$") margin at the upper edge of the front roof piece and

2mm ($^1/_8$") margins at the remaining upper and lower edges (*diag 18*).

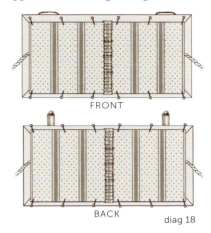

FRONT

BACK

diag 18

Ladder stitch the upper edge of the lining to the roof seam allowance (*diag 19*).

diag 19

Ladder stitch the short ends, securing the cord stays in the stitching. Ladder stitch the lower edge in place in the same manner.

12. Attaching the roof

Pin the roof in position and ladder stitch to the walls on the outside.

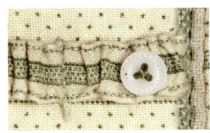

COVERED ELASTIC BAND

TWISTED CORD ROOF STAYS

Liftout tray

13. Constructing the outer tray

Lace and mitre the fabric pieces over the corresponding mountboard pieces in the same manner as the outer walls of the house box, ensuring the fabric print is aligned on each piece.

Ladder stitch the outer tray together in the same manner as the house box walls. Insert the base and ladder stitch the walls to the base.

14. Constructing the inner tray

Attach the felt padding to the four inner base pieces and trim flush with the mountboard in the same manner as before.

Lace and mitre the fabric pieces for the inner tray walls and bases over the corresponding mountboard pieces as before, ensuring the fabric print is aligned on each piece.

Stitch the inner tray walls together from the wrong side in the same manner as the box lining.

15. Preparing the dividers

It is important to complete each divider in numerical order so that each can be secured to its neighbour.

Referring to the diagram for placement, position the interfacing and mountboard for divider (D1) on the wrong side of the corresponding fabric piece, leaving a 1mm ($1/32$") gap between the pieces. Fuse the interfacing in place (*diag 20*).

diag 20

Fold the corners of the fabric to the wrong side, over the mountboard and interfacing, and press (*diag 21*).

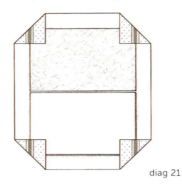

diag 21

Press the seam allowance of the fabric over the mountboard and the interfacing. Lace the fabric from side to side over the mountboard only and ladder stitch the two mitred corners at the mountboard end (*diag 22*).

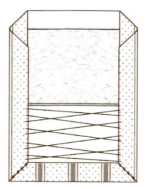

diag 22

Fold the remaining seam allowance to the wrong side over the interfacing and press in place.

16. Assembling the dividers

Divider (D1)

With wrong sides together, fold the interfaced half of the fabric over the mountboard and pin. Ladder stitch the three edges together.

On each short end, mark the centre and 5mm ($3/16$") from the upper and lower edges. Cut three generous lengths of quilting thread. Using a long needle, pass each thread through the divider between the layers at each marked position (*diag 23*).

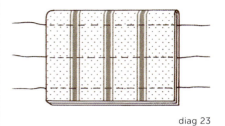

diag 23

Divider (D2)

Prepare divider (D2) according to step 15, making sure the interfaced half of the fabric is still unfolded.

With the mountboard facing up, measure 3.8cm ($1 1/2$") from the left hand end of divider (D2) and mark three points matching the measurements for divider (D1) (*diag 24*).

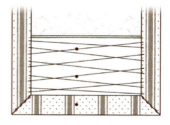

diag 24

Use a heavy needle to pierce a hole at each mark.

Thread up each quilting thread of divider (D1) and pass it from the right side through its corresponding hole, making sure to leave the interfaced half of divider (D2) free (*diag 25*).

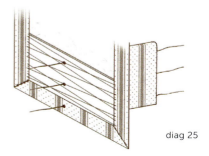

diag 25

Tie the ends firmly together with a double parcel knot – left over right, left over right again, then right over left – to form a knot that won't slip (*diag 26*).

HINT *Checking measurements*

I recommend you tack the outer tray together roughly and check it slides in and out of the box easily. I did not and had to undo twelve hours of work to shave 1mm ($1/32$") off the edge of each piece!

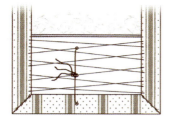

diag 26

Trim the tied tails, leaving the opposite ends free.

Fold the interfaced half down and ladder stitch the three edges of divider (D2) in the same manner as (D1). Measure and pass three lengths of quilting thread between the layers of divider (D2) as for (D1).

Divider (D3)

Prepare divider (D3) according to step 15. Measure halfway along the divider (D3) and mark the three points for the holes as before. Pierce a hole at each mark and thread the corresponding quilting thread tails of divider (D2) through the holes.

Securely tie the thread tails with a double parcel knot. Fold the interfaced fabric down and ladder stitch the three sides as before (diag 27).

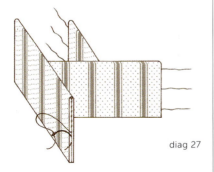

diag 27

Measure and pass three lengths of quilting thread between the layers of the divider as before.

17. Attaching the dividers to the tray lining

Slide the dividers into the inner tray to confirm the fit and adjust the

measurements if necessary. Mark the points where the dividers meet the inner tray, then remove the dividers. Measure and pierce three holes as before at each marked position (diag 28).

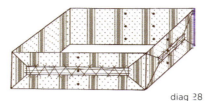

diag 28

Position the dividers inside the inner tray walls and thread the remaining tails of divider D1 through the corresponding holes. Pull taut and tie with a double parcel knot. Do not trim the tails yet. Secure the remaining two dividers in the same manner.

Insert each base into its compartment. Pin and ladder stitch on the wrong side. Re-tension the quilting threads if necessary and trim the tails.

Using matching machine sewing thread, secure the top edge of each divider to its adjacent wall, ladder stitching in a square pattern a number of times (diag 29).

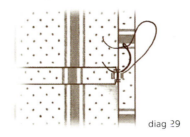

diag 29

18. Making the twisted cord handles

Cut three, 45cm (17¾") lengths of B3 for each handle. Knot the ends and make a twisted cord. Wrap the cord tightly using one strand of the same thread. Take a few stitches through the wraps to secure.

19. Completing the inner tray

On one short end of the inner tray, measure and mark 2cm (¾") from each

corner. Leaving a 7cm (2¾") loop at the upper edge, secure a cord to the upper and lower seam allowances (diag 30).

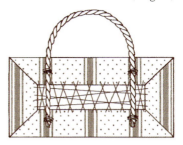

diag 30

Repeat for the remaining cord at the other end of the tray. Insert the inner tray into the outer tray and ladder stitch around the upper edge (diag 31).

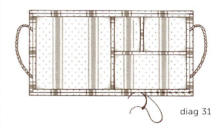

diag 31

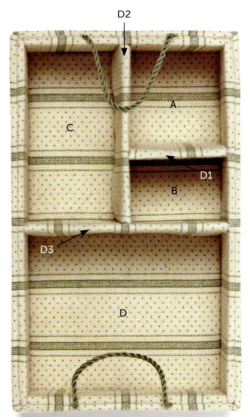

LIFTOUT TRAY

Accessories

Requirements

Fabric

50cm x 120cm wide (20" x 48") of natural cotton–linen blend will accommodate all accessory pieces.

Cutting layout

Natural cotton–linen blend

1. Emery block – page 46
2. Needlebook – page 49
3. Pincushion – page 56
4. Scissor keep – page 59
5. Spool holder – page 62
6. Tape measure cover – page 68
7. Thimble holder – page 72
8. Thread cutter cover – page 78

1	3	4	8	
2	5	6	7

See the individual projects for remaining requirements.

Equipment

10cm (4") deep sided embroidery hoop, inner ring bound

15cm (6") deep sided embroidery hoop, inner ring bound

20cm (8") deep sided embroidery hoop, inner ring bound

Small piece of lightweight interfacing for templates

Small screwdriver

Berry pins

Set square

Metal ruler

Cutting mat

Sharp craft knife

PVA glue

Small paintbrush

Sticky tape

Double sided tape

Sharp dressmaker's scissors

Pinking shears

Paper scissors

Fine sandpaper

Tracing paper

Lightweight paper, e.g. airmail paper

Fine water-soluble pen

Fine black pen

Fine 01 (0.25mm) brown acid free permanent pen, e.g. Pigma

Mechanical pencil

Threads

See page 11 for the complete thread list. Refer to the individual projects for thread use.

Needles

Refer to the needle chart on page 10.

Preparation for embroidery

The fabric pieces required for the accessories are all prepared in the same manner.

Prepare the fabric by neatening the raw edges with an overlock or machine zigzag stitch to prevent fraying.

For the pieces that are cut out using a template, use the black pen to trace the dashed outline and placement marks for the piece onto lightweight interfacing. Cut this out to make a template. Aligning the placement marks with the straight grain of the cotton–linen, centre the template onto the fabric, leaving ample space around it for seam allowances. Tack around the outline of the shape using pale coloured machine sewing thread, then remove the template.

For square and rectangular pieces, tack the outline along the grain of the fabric, following the measurements given in the individual instructions.

Transfer the embroidery designs following the instructions for the house box on page 9.

Bee emery block

Today emery cushions for sharpening needles are often created in the shape of strawberries, but traditionally they were cylindrical cushions with wide bands around the middle made of wood, metal or even intricately carved ivory. This petite embroidered emery block features a fat bumblebee humming lazily over cheerful spring blossoms.

The emery block measures 3.2cm x 2.6cm wide (1¼" x 1").

FRONT

BACK

Requirements

Fabric

20cm (8") square of natural cotton–linen blend

Supplies

20cm x 6mm wide (8" x ¼") piece of lime green and white ribbon

Emery felt strawberry

5cm x 8cm wide (2" x 3⅛") piece of template plastic

5cm x 10cm wide (2" x 4") piece of lightweight fusible wadding, e.g. Pellon

5cm x 10cm wide (2" x 4") piece of firm, medium weight wadding, e.g. Ultrafleece

Quilting thread

Equipment

See page 44.

NEEDLES

Refer to the needle chart on page 10.

No. 9 betweens

No. 9 crewel

No. 26 tapestry

THREADS

Refer to the combined list of threads on page 11.

Au Papillon Fil d'Or deluxe
B

Au Ver à Soie Antique Metallics
D

Au Ver à Soie, Soie d'Alger
I

Caron Soie Cristale stranded silk
L, M, N

Colour Streams Silken Strands
V

DMC stranded cotton
AA, AE, AH

Weeks Dye Works stranded cotton
BE

YLI fine metallic
BK

Preparation for embroidery

See the liftout pattern for the embroidery designs.

Prepare the fabric following the instructions on page 44, tacking two rectangles, each 2.5cm x 3cm wide (1" x 1³⁄₁₆") for the front and back, leaving 3cm (1³⁄₁₆") between for seam allowances *(diag 1)*.

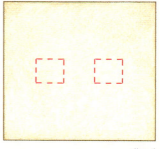

diag 1

Aligning the tacking with the dashed outlines, transfer the embroidery designs and cutting lines following the instructions on page 9.

Embroidery

All embroidery is worked with the fabric held taut in the hoop, using the needle in a stabbing motion.

Refer to the close-up photograph and embroidery key for colour placement.

Order of work

Refer to the step-by-step instructions for raised cross stitch on page 95 and trellis stich on page 98.

BEE

Body

Using two strands of B, outline the body in small back stitches. Rotate the work, so the base of the body is towards you. Change to the tapestry needle and work six trellis stitches into six back stitches across the base of the body (*diag 2*).

Continue to fill the body with trellis stitch, anchoring each row onto the back stitches. If necessary, increase a stitch at each end of a couple of rows to cover the wider part of the body. As the body becomes narrower, gradually decrease to one stitch.

Thorax and head

Work three small satin stitches across the upper end of the body for the thorax, and work another two stitches over the top (*diag 3*).

diag 3

Using the same thread, work a colonial knot for the head.

Wings

Using BK, bring the thread to the front next to the thorax, just behind the head. Work a detached chain and,

without anchoring the stitch continue to embroider the wing in blanket stitch (*diag 4*).

diag 4

Legs and Antennae

Using D, embroider three straight stitches for each leg and a straight stitch for each antenna.

FIELD FLOWERS AND GRASS

Grass

Using two strands of BE, work straight stitches of differing lengths and angles 5mm (³/₁₆") from the lower tacked line on the front, and at the marked positions on the back. To lessen the risk of puckering and decrease the amount of thread on the back, work the stitches as shown (*diag 5*).

diag 5

Pink anemones

Referring to the close-up photographs for colour placement, work a raised cross stitch at the position of each flower, using two strands of L, M or N. Work a colonial knot at the centre of each flower using two strands of AA.

Cream daisies

Stitch three detached chains for the petals, with two strands of AE, working the centre stitch first. Change to V and work a colonial knot for the flower centre.

Blue forget-me-nots

Using two strands of I, stitch a granitos for each petal. For each granitos work three stitches into the same holes. Leave a tiny space in the centre (*diag 6*).

diag 6

Change to two strands of V and work a colonial knot for the flower centre.

Using I, stitch pairs of colonial knots among the flowers for the tiny buds, adding a French knot above each pair.

EMBROIDERY KEY

All embroidery is worked using one strand of thread unless otherwise specified.

Bee

Body, thorax and head = B
(2 strands, back stitch, trellis stitch, satin stitch, colonial knot)

Wings = BK
(detached chain stitch, blanket stitch)

Legs and antennae = D
(straight stitch)

Field flowers and grass

Grass = BE (2 strands, straight stitch)

Pink anemone = L, M or N
(2 strands, raised cross stitch),
AA (2 strands, colonial knot)

Cream daisies = AE
(2 strands, detached chain),
V (2 strands, colonial knot)

Blue forget-me-nots = I
(2 strands, granitos, 3 stitches),
V (2 strands, colonial knot)

Tiny buds = I (2 strands, colonial knot, French knot)

Construction

The shaded areas in the following diagrams indicate the right side of the fabric.

Cutting out

Cut the pieces following the measurements below.

Lightweight fusible wadding

Cut two, each 2.5cm x 3cm wide (1" x 1¼")

Cut two, each 3.5cm x 4cm wide (1³⁄₈" x 1³⁄₁₆")

Firm, medium weight wadding

Cut two, each 3cm x 3.5cm wide (1¼" x 1³⁄₈").

Template plastic

Cut two, each 2.5cm x 3cm wide (1" x 1¼")

Order of work

Refer to the step-by-step instructions for glove stitch on page 87 and lacing and mitring corners over mountboard on page 88.

1. Preparing the embroidered piece

Block the embroidery following the instructions on page 37. Cut out along the marked cutting lines.

2. Preparing the front and back pieces

Apply a small amount of glue at each corner of one piece of template plastic. Glue one of the smaller pieces of lightweight fusible wadding in place, with the fusible side facing upwards (*diag 1*).

diag 1

Centre a piece of medium weight wadding over the fusible wadding. Fuse in place, protecting your iron with a sheet of baking paper.

Fuse one of the larger pieces of fusible lightweight wadding to the wrong

side of the embroidered front piece, centring the wadding over the tacking (*diag 2*).

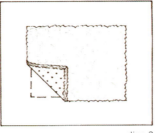

diag 2

With the plastic facing up, position the prepared template plastic on the wrong side of the backed embroidered piece (*diag 3*).

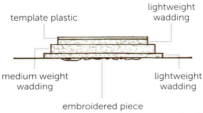

template plastic   lightweight wadding

medium weight wadding   lightweight wadding

embroidered piece

diag 3

Pin the fabric onto the covered plastic at the midpoint on all four sides, pushing the pins into the wadding. Then pin on each side of the midpoint (*diag 4*).

diag 4

Starting and finishing 1.5cm (⁵⁄₈") from the short ends, lace the seam allowances and mitre the corners over the plastic. Remove the tacking.

Repeat for the back embroidered piece.

Assembling the emery block

Cut a 15cm (6") length of lime green ribbon. Fold 1cm (³⁄₈") under at one end.

With wrong sides together and starting with the folded ribbon end at the lower

right corner, glove stitch the ribbon to the front piece using two strands of AH (*diag 5*).

diag 5

Matching corners and ensuring correct orientation, stitch the back piece to the other edge of the ribbon, leaving one short end of the emery block open (*diag 6*).

diag 6

Use a small funnel to fill your emery firmly with the emery powder from the felt strawberry, using the eye of a heavy needle to poke it into the corners of the emery block.

Finish glove stitching the ribbon in place. Turn under the remaining end of the ribbon and ladder stitch the folded edges of the ribbon together with matching machine sewing thread.

Pea needlebook

Since the dawn of time, needleworkers have looked for ornamental ways to keep their treasured needles safe. An archaeological investigation in Sweden even found bone needlecases dating back to 6000 BC. Stitched onto natural cotton and linen, with a dainty embroidered pea vine nestled between cottage garden flowers and a lazy snail on the cover, this gorgeous needlebook is a delightful way to continue the tradition.

The needlebook measures 7.6cm x 6.2cm wide (3" x 2 7/16").

Requirements

Fabric

30cm (12") square of natural cotton–linen blend

12cm x 16cm wide (4 3/4" x 6 1/4") piece of pale butter and fern green print cotton

10cm x 30cm wide (4" x 12") piece of ivory doctor's flannel

Small piece of brown wool felt

Supplies

10cm x 15cm wide (4" x 6") piece of lightweight fusible interfacing

10cm x 15cm wide (4" x 6") piece of lightweight fusible wadding, e.g. Pellon

5cm (2") square of appliqué paper

10cm x 15cm wide (4" x 6") piece of 1.2mm (3/32") acid-free mountboard

Fine grey beading thread, e.g. Nymo

Quilting thread

Matching machine sewing thread

Beads

1 x 6mm (1/4") green nephrite bead

Equipment

See page 44

NEEDLES

Refer to the needle chart on page 10.

No. 9 betweens

No. 8 crewel

No. 9 crewel

No. 10 crewel

No. 26 tapestry

THREADS & BEADS

Refer to the combined list of threads on page 11.

Au Papillon Fil d'Or deluxe

A, B

Au Ver à Soie Antique Metallics

D

Au Ver à Soie, Soie d'Alger

G, H, I

Caron Soie Cristale stranded silk

L, M, O, P

Colour Streams Silken Strands

S, U, V

DMC stranded cotton

Z, AA, AE, AH

Gumnut Yarns 'Stars' stranded silk

AR, AT

Threadworx stranded variegated cotton

BC

Weeks Dye Works stranded cotton

BE

YLI silk floss

BF, BH

Beads

Mill Hill petite seed beads

BO, BP

Non-branded craft beads and sequins

BQ, BR

Preparation for embroidery

See the liftout pattern for the embroidery design.

Prepare the fabric referring to the instructions on page 44, tacking a 7.6cm x 13cm wide (3" x 5¼") rectangle to mark the outlines of the needlecase cover at the centre of the cotton–linen piece.

Aligning the tacking with the dashed outlines, transfer the embroidery designs and cutting lines following the instructions on page 9, marking the corners of the two inner solid borders with pins.

Removing the pins as you go, tack from pin to pin with pale coloured machine sewing thread, following the grain of the fabric (*diag 1*).

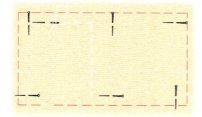

diag 1

Embroidery

See the liftout pattern for the snail shell templates.

All embroidery is worked with the fabric held taut in the hoop, using the needle in a stabbing motion.

Refer to the close-up photograph and embroidery key for colour placement.

Order of work

PEA

Refer to the step-by-step instructions for working Hungarian braided chain stitch on page 87 and interlaced chain stitch on page 88.

Main Stem

Working from the base to the tip, embroider the stem in Hungarian braided chain stitch using two strands of P. Using B in the fine tapestry needle, whip around the inside chains only (*diag 2*).

diag 2

Leaf stalk

Stitching from the base, work the stalk in coral stitch using two strands of P, placing the knots close together. Work a row of outline stitch along the right hand side of the stalk with O. Changing to D, whip the outline stitches in the same direction (*diag 3*).

diag 3

Tendrils

Embroider the tendrils in stem stitch with P, keeping the stitches short to follow the tight curves.

Pea pod

Work the centre of the pea with interlaced chain stitch. Using two strands of P, begin at the top and embroider a row of large chain stitches along the centre to the tip of the pea.

Lace each side of the chain stitches loosely using three strands of A in the tapestry needle, working each row from the top to the tip. Change to one strand of the same thread and couch the lacing thread at the outermost points to pull it slightly open.

Using the beading thread, attach a sequin (BR) with a tiny bead (BP) inside each chain.

Changing to two strands of P, outline the pea in whipped chain stitch, working each side from the top to the tip of the pea.

Sepals

Outline each sepal with tiny split back stitches using P. Fill the shape with horizontal satin stitches, working within the outline.

Starting in the middle of the upper section of the sepal, work long and short stitch towards one side using O. Bring the thread to the front inside the shape and take the needle to the back just outside the outline, angling the needle back towards the sepal. Fan out the direction of the stitches to follow the shape (*diag 4*).

diag 4

Return to the halfway point and work long and short stitch across the remaining side in the same manner. Change to P and cover the lower section of the sepal in long and short stitch, bringing the needle to the front through the previous stitches and to the back outside the outline. Where required, work two rows of shorter stitches so they follow the curve of the sepal.

Pea Flower

Using S, work split back stitch along the outer edge of the centre petal. Outline the two side petals in a similar manner using H and the base petal using Z. Changing back to H, pad the two outer petals with satin stitch worked across each shape inside the outline.

Covering the outline, fill the centre petal with long and short stitch using S. Changing to Z, cover the tiny petal at the base of the flower with satin stitch worked along the length of the petal (*diag 5*).

diag 5

Embroider the side petals in a similar manner to the centre petal using H and angling the direction of the stitches towards the stalk.

Work the highlights on the centre petal in straight stitches using BH and on the side petals using BF.

Sepals

Outline the sepals in tiny split back stitches with P. Using the same thread, stitch three layers of satin stitch padding within the outline. Work the first layer across the shape a short distance from the outline, followed by a second layer along the length of the shape. Stitch the final layer across the width, working just inside the outline (*diag 6*).

diag 6

Starting midway along the upper half of the sepal, work long and short stitch to one side, covering the outline and angling your stitches towards the stalk. Return to the centre and work across to the opposite side in the same manner. Cover the remaining half of the sepal, splitting the previous stitches.

Leaf

Outline the leaf with small split back stitches using AR. Embroider the outer edge of the leaf in long and short stitch with the same thread, working each stitch from inside the shape and over the outline. Gradually change the angle of the stitches to follow the direction of the veins.

Thread one strand each of G and O into separate needles and work the second row of long and short stitch, splitting the stitches in the previous row and changing between the two needles. The greater the difference between the tones of green, the more staggered the boundary should be between them. Work a few stitches with one thread, leave a space or two, then work a few

with the other tone. Always leave the spare thread on top of your work, so it will not get caught.

Leave a narrow space down the middle of the leaf for the vein. Stitching from the base towards the tip of the leaf, work the centre vein in stem stitch with U. Embroider long straight stitches for the veins using the same thread. Change to D and work straight stitch highlights along the veins.

SNAIL

Refer to the step-by-step instructions for working ladder stitch on page 90.

Shell

Outline the shell in split back stitch with BC.

Trace the shell templates onto appliqué paper. With the paper side uppermost, fuse the tracing to a small piece of brown wool felt and cut out along the marked lines. Remove the paper backing. Centre the smallest piece inside the shell outline and secure with stab stitches using matching machine sewing thread. Position and secure the larger piece over the top. Draw the spiral of the shell on the felt with the pencil (*diag 7*).

diag 7

FRONT

Body and tail

Beginning near the shell, work straight stitch bars across the body at 2.5mm ($^{11}/_{16}$") intervals, using BC.

Change to the fine tapestry needle. Emerge at the lower edge of the body, near the head.

Work raised stem stitch into the bars, working each row from the head to the shell, pushing them close together.

Embroider the tail in a similar manner, bringing the needle out from under the shell and working towards the tip. To achieve a nice point for the tail, finish each row a needle width further out from the point (*diag 10*).

diag 10

To complete the shell, work outline stitch along the lower edge of the shell, and the purl edge of the spiralling upper section with D.

Antennae and eyes

Work a long straight stitch for each antenna using D. Stitch a bead (BO) in place with fine beading thread at the top of each for the eyes.

LADYBIRD

Body

Outline the body with split back stitch using AT. Pad the body with three layers of satin stitch within the outline using the same thread. Each layer of stitches is in the opposite direction to the previous.

Covering the outline, embroider the final layer of satin stitch along the length of the body, beginning at the centre and stitching one side at a time. Bring the needle to the front at an angle from under the outline on one side and take it to the back at an angle on the other, so that the stitches hug the split back stitch.

Using two strands of BC, cover the lower section of the shell with ladder stitch. To accommodate the curve of the shell, alter the width of the ladder stitch and increase the spacing between the stitches along the lower edge to ensure all stitches are at a right angle to the outline (*diag 8*).

diag 8

Using the same thread, stitch a row of raised chain band along the centre of the ladder stitch.

Starting at the centre of the spiral, work short blanket stitches into the same hole at the top. As you near the completion of the first round, continue around the shape by gradually increasing the spacing of the stitches along the outer edge and working the inside edge closely against the first round of stitches to form a spiral (*diag 9*).

diag 9

Changing to AA, scatter nine seed stitches over the body for the spots. Take care not to pull too tightly and disturb the underlying satin stitches.

Head

Outline the head in split back stitch with AA. Embroider four or five satin stitches across the head, covering the outline. Work a small straight stitch for each antenna.

Legs

Work two front legs at the junction of the head and body, and two legs evenly spaced along each side of the body using AA. Stitch three short straight stitches for each leg to achieve the correct shape *(diag 11)*.

diag 11

FIELD FLOWERS AND GRASS

Refer to the step-by-step instructions for raised cross stitch on page 95.

The flowers and grass on the needlebook front and back are embroidered in a similar manner.

Grass

Using two strands of AH or BE work straight stitches of differing lengths and angles 5mm (³/₁₆") from the lower tacked line. To lessen the risk of puckering and decrease the amount of thread on the back, work the stitches as shown *(diag 12)*.

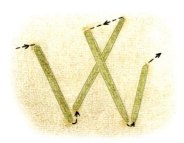

diag 12

BACK

Dill weed

To embroider the dill weed, work the stems in stem stitch and fly stitch with BE. Embroider the flower head with five to seven pistil stitches of varying lengths, fanning out from the top of the stem.

Pink anemones

Referring to the close-up photographs for colour placement, work a raised cross stitch at the position of each flower, using two strands of L or M.

Work a colonial knot at the centre of each flower using two strands of AA.

Cream daisies

Stitch three detached chains for the petals, with two strands of AE, working the centre stitch first. Change to V and work a colonial knot for the flower centre.

Blue forget-me-nots

Using two strands of I, stitch a granitos for each petal. For each granitos work three stitches into the same holes. Leave a tiny space in the centre *(diag 13)*.

diag 13

Change to two strands of V and work a colonial knot for the flower centre.

Using I, stitch pairs of colonial knots among the flowers for the tiny buds.

Border

Using two strands of O, embroider the border in chain stitch. Start at the lower left hand corner and work the lower edge, then the right hand side. Start again at the lower left corner, work the left hand side, then the upper edge. This way, your chain stitches face the same way on each side (*diag 14*).

diag 14

Embroider a row of stem stitch with two strands of A along the outside of the chain stitch.

EMBROIDERY KEY

All embroidery is worked with one strand of thread unless otherwise specified.

Pea

Main stem = P (2 strands, Hungarian braided chain stitch), B (whipping)

Leaf stalk = P (2 strands, coral stitch), O (outline stitch), D (whipping)

Tendrils = P (stem stitch)

Pea pod = P (2 strands, chain stitch), A (3 strands, lacing), A (couching), BR and BP (beading), P (2 strands, chain stitch, whipping)

Sepals = P (split back stitch, padded satin stitch), O or P (long and short stitch)

Pea Flower

Petals = H, S or Z (split back stitch, padded satin stitch, satin stitch, long and short stitch), BF or BH (straight stitch)

Sepals = P (split back stitch, padded satin stitch, long and short stitch)

Leaf = AR (split back stitch, long and short stitch), G and O (long and short stitch), U (stem stitch, straight stitch), D (straight stitch)

Snail

Shell = BC (split back stitch), (2 strands, ladder stitch, raised chain band, blanket stitch), D (outline stitch)

Body and tail = BC (straight stitch, raised stem stitch)

Antennae and eyes = D (straight stitch), BO (beading)

Ladybird

Body = AT (split back stitch, padded satin stitch, satin stitch), AA (seed stitch)

Head = AA (split back stitch, satin stitch)

Antennae and legs = AA (straight stitch)

Field flowers and grass

Grass = AH or BE (2 strands, straight stitch)

Dill weed = BE (straight stitch, pistil stitch)

Pink anemones = L or M (2 strands, raised cross stitch), AA (2 strands, colonial knot)

Cream daisies = AE (2 strands, detached chain stitch), V (2 strands, colonial knot)

Blue forget-me-nots = I (2 strands, granitos), V (2 strands, colonial knot)

Buds = I (2 strands, colonial knot)

Border = O (2 strands, chain stitch), A (2 strands, stem stitch)

NEEDLEBOOK INTERIOR

Construction

The shaded areas in the following diagrams indicate the right side of the fabric.

Cutting out

See the liftout pattern for the templates.

Where templates are not provided, cut the pieces according to the measurements below.

Doctor's flannel

Needle pages: cut one, 7cm x 11.4cm wide (2³⁄₄" x 4¹⁄₂") using pinking shears

Needle pages: cut one, 7cm x 11.2cm wide (2³⁄₄" x 4³⁄₈") using pinking shears

Lightweight fusible interfacing

Cut one, 7.3cm x 12.4cm wide (2⁷⁄₈" x 4⁷⁄₈")

Order of work

Refer to the step-by-step instructions for lacing and mitring corners over mountboard on page 88, Palestrina knot on page 92 and up and down blanket stitch loop on page 99.

1. Preparing the embroidered piece

Block and press the embroidered fabric following the instructions on page 37. Cut out along the marked cutting lines.

2. Preparing the mountboard

Measure and mark the midpoint on one long edge. Measure out and mark 2.5mm (¹⁄₈") on each side of the midpoint and draw a vertical line at each mark. Score along these lines, cutting through the paper layer only (*diag 1*).

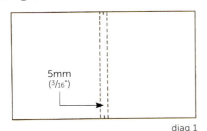

5mm
(³⁄₁₆")

diag 1

Bend the cardboard along each score line for the spine.

Measure and mark 6.1cm (2³⁄₈") from each score line and draw two vertical lines at the marked points. Measure and mark 7.6cm (3") from one long edge and draw a horizontal line at the marked point (*diag 2*).

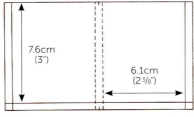

7.6cm
(3")

6.1cm
(2³⁄₈")

diag 2

Recut the mountboard piece to size along the marked lines and sand any rough spots if necessary.

3. Making the cover

Cut a piece of lightweight wadding 5mm (³⁄₁₆") larger than the mountboard piece on all four sides. Apply a dot of glue to each corner of the piece using a small paintbrush.

Position the wadding over the mountboard and press lightly at the corners to secure. Leave to dry.

Trim along all edges, leaving a 2.5mm (¹⁄₈") margin of wadding on all four sides.

Position the embroidered panel over the wadding. With the embroidered side facing you to ensure the border is straight, secure with pins pushed into the mountboard edge around all sides at 1cm (³⁄₈") intervals, gently stretching the fabric taut.

Lace the fabric over the mountboard and mitre the corners.

4. Preparing the lining

Centre the interfacing over the wrong side of the lining piece and fuse in place. Fold and press the lining seam

allowances over the interfacing. Unfold. Fold each corner to the wrong side over the interfacing and press. Refold the seam allowances along each side to mitre the corners (*diag 3*).

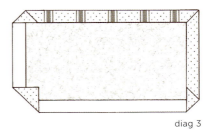

diag 3

Tack the seam allowances to the interfacing. Measure and mark the midpoint on each long edge of the lining piece with a pin.

5. Attaching the needle pages

Place the two flannel pages together, with the shorter piece on top. Pin in position on the right side of the lining. Machine stitch in place along the centre using matching machine sewing thread and with the stitch length set to 3mm (¹⁄₈").

Using 2 strands of O, work Palestrina stitch over the machine stitches, keeping the spacing even.

6. Attaching the lining and pages

Centre the prepared lining and needle pages over the inside of the needlebook. Pin and ladder stitch in place. Remove any visible tacking stitches.

7. Finishing

Using matching thread, stitch the green nephrite bead securely in place at the centre back opening edge. Following the step-by-step instructions, work an up and down blanket stitch loop to match at the centre of the front opening edge, using three strands of O.

Rose pincushion

NEEDLES

Refer to the needle chart on page 10.

No. 8 crewel

No. 9 crewel

No. 10 crewel

No. 7 milliner's

THREADS & BEADS

Refer to the combined list of threads on page 11.

Caron Soie Cristale stranded silk
N, O

Colour Streams Silken Strands
S

DMC no. 8 perlé cotton
X

DMC stranded cotton
AH, AI

Gumnut Yarns 'Stars' stranded silk
AS

Beads

Mill Hill petite seed beads
BP

Pincushions became popular in the seventeenth century, when they sat on the dressing table and held large, decorative clothing pins. Later they became an important part of sewing kits, and incorporated different features including wax spools used to smooth thread, and clamps to screw the pincushion to table edges or chair arms. This enchanting little pincushion, adorned with a garland of miniature roses, is the perfect size to slip in your workbox.

The pincushion measures 5.7cm (2 ¹/₄") in diameter.

Requirements

Fabric

20cm (8") square of natural cotton–linen blend

Supplies

10cm x 20cm wide (4" x 8") piece of lightweight wadding, e.g. Pellon

2 x 6mm (¹/₄") mother of pearl buttons

Matching machine sewing thread

Equipment

See page 44.

Preparation for embroidery

See the liftout pattern for the embroidery design.

Prepare the fabric referring to the instructions on page 44.

Align the tacking with the dashed outline and transfer the front embroidery design and cutting line following the instructions on page 9. Mark the centre and segments with the water-soluble fabric marker. Repeat for the back.

Embroidery

All embroidery is worked with the fabric held taut in the hoop, using the needle in a stabbing motion, except for the rosette stitch.

Refer to the close-up photograph and embroidery key for colour placement.

Order of work

Refer to the step-by-step instructions for working rosette stitch on page 96.

Vine

Using two strands of AS, embroider the vine in stem stitch.

Roses

Embroider the roses in rosette stitch using three strands of N or S. Add a colonial knot in the same colour at the centre of each flower.

Work the rosebuds in fishbone stitch using two strands of N or S, stitching each from the tip to halfway along the marked line *(diag 1)*.

diag 1

Change to two strands of AS and work three or four stitches for the sepal, gradually shaping the sepal inwards to the stem.

Leaves

Embroider the leaves using AH, AI or AS, referring to page 14 for hints on working the leaves. Beginning at the tip, stitch an uneven fly stitch – short on one side, long on the other. For a leaf curving to the left, bring the thread to the front at (a), take it to the back at (b) and emerge at (c) to anchor the stitch *(diag 2)*.

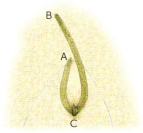

diag 2

For a leaf curving to the right, (a) should be above (b) *(diag 3)*.

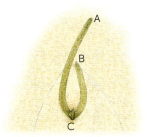

diag 3

Work fly stitches close together, gradually increasing the width of the stitches to shape the leaf.

When the leaf is broad enough, gradually decrease the width of the stitches.

The anchoring stitches should line up neatly to make the mid rib of the leaf *(diag 4)*.

diag 4

Try to keep the leaves within each marked segment to avoid distorting the embroidery when the pincushion is laced.

Construction

The shaded areas in the following diagrams indicate the right side of the fabric.

Cutting out

See the liftout pattern for the templates.

Cut out two pieces of wadding using the pincushion back as a template.

Order of work

Refer to the step-by-step instructions for beaded Hedebo edge on page 83.

1. Preparing the front and back

Block and press the embroidered fabric following the instructions on page 37. Machine staystitch on the stitchline along the opening on both the front and back pieces as indicated on the pattern. Cut out each circle along the marked cutting lines. Pin a lightweight wadding piece to the wrong side of each fabric circle.

2. Making the pincushion

With right sides facing and matching grain lines, pin the front and back

Orts

The little pumpkin pincushion is stuffed with 'orts'. Orts are snipped up pieces of cotton or silk threads – no need to feel guilty about unpicking and wasting thread ever again! To stuff the orts I use a teddy bear stuffing tool or a chopstick. If you have a handy husband, ask him to taper a wooden chopstick at one end to make it slimmer and more rounded.

Machine stitching curved seams

Use a small stitch length – this gives a smoother seamline when turned to the right side.

4. Edge

Stitch a beaded Hedebo edge along the seamline of the pincushion, completing one segment at a time.

Using two strands of O and starting with a small cross stitch, work the foundation for three scallops in a segment (*diag 4*).

diag 4

Work the Hedebo stitch using the same thread and attach a bead (BP) between each scallop.

Work the foundation for three scallops in the next segment, alternating the order of long and short cross stitches, so that there is only one bead on each lacing thread (*diag 5*).

diag 5

circles together. Tack along the stitchline. Machine stitch, leaving an opening along the staystitching (*diag 1*).

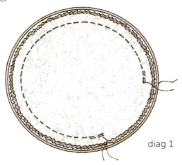

diag 1

Trim the wadding close to the machine stitching and remove all tacking. Clip the seam allowance at 1cm (³⁄₈") intervals. Turn to the right side through the opening. Stuff the pincushion firmly with 'orts'. Ladder stitch the opening closed.

3. Lacing the pincushion

Thread a 1m (39") length of X into the milliner's needle. Knot the end of the thread.

Take the needle from centre back to centre front. Tug your thread to 'pop' the knot to the inside. Loop the thread over the edge of the pincushion and take the needle from centre back to centre front. Position the thread along the grain of the fabric at a marked

segment line and pull taut, to make the edge of the pincushion dimple (*diag 2*).

diag 2

Repeat at each quarter mark, following the grain of the fabric, then place a stitch halfway between each in a similar manner to form the eight segments (*diag 3*).

diag 3

Secure the thread at the centre, but do not trim. Using the same thread, attach a small mother of pearl button in the centre of the front and back.

Finishing threads

Work a small back stitch in the ditch of the seam. Take the thread through the pincushion. Pull it taut and trim close to the fabric. The thread tail will spring back into the pincushion.

PINCUSHION BASE

Strawberry flower scissor keep

Although scissors have been around since ancient times, modern scissors weren't invented until the eighteenth century. Women would often hang them from their chatelaines, along with keys and other embroidery tools. Decorated with a single strawberry flower and embroidered initial stitched onto natural linen, this elegant scissor keep is finished with colourful beads and a lustrous green twisted cord to ensure your embroidery scissors will always be easy to find.

The scissor keep measures 3.2cm (1 1/4") square.

Requirements

Fabric

20cm (8") square of natural cotton–linen blend

Supplies

6cm x 4cm wide (2 3/8" x 1 1/2") piece of lightweight fusible wadding, e.g Pellon

5cm x 10cm wide (2" x 4") piece of stiff interfacing, e.g. buckram

2cm (3/4") square curtain weight

Small piece of cotton tape

Quilting thread

Matching machine sewing thread

Beads

1 x 6mm (1/4") dark green lamp bead with pink flowers

2 x 4mm (3/16") green frosted glass beads

2 x 4mm (3/16") brass spacer beads

Equipment

See page 44.

NEEDLES

Refer to the needle chart on page 10.

No. 9 between

No. 8 crewel

No. 9 crewel

No. 10 crewel

THREADS & BEADS

Refer to the combined list of threads on page 11.

Au Papillon Fil d'Or deluxe
B

Au Ver à Soie, Soie d'Alger
K

Caron Soie Cristale stranded silk
O

Colour Streams Silken Strands
T

Gumnut Yarns 'Stars' stranded silk
AR

Rajmahal stranded rayon
AY

Beads

Mill Hill seed beads
BM

Preparation for embroidery

See the liftout pattern for the embroidery design and alphabet.

Prepare the fabric referring to the instructions on page 44, tacking a 3cm x 6cm wide (1³/₁₆" x 2³/₈") rectangle to mark the outlines of the scissor keep at the centre of the cotton–linen piece.

Centring your chosen initial on the back of the design, transfer the embroidery design and cutting lines following the instructions on page 9, marking the corners of the front and back inner solid borders with pins.

Removing the pins as you go, tack from pin to pin with pale coloured machine sewing thread, following the grain of the fabric *(diag 1)*.

diag 1

Embroidery

All embroidery is worked with the fabric held taut in the hoop, using the needle in a stabbing motion.

Refer to the close-up photographs and embroidery key for colour placement.

Order of work

STRAWBERRY FLOWER

Outline the petals in split back stitch using K, stitching a single row between the petals and around the flower centre *(diag 2)*.

diag 2

Using the same thread, work two layers of satin stitch padding, ensuring the uppermost layer is worked across the width of the petals. Embroider satin stitch over the padding, bringing the thread to the front on the outer edge of the petal and taking the needle to the back over the outline on the inner edge. If your stitches become too crowded, work some ³/₄ length stitches.

Changing to AR, work a straight stitch to mark the divisions between the petals. Embroider three straight stitches of varying lengths over each petal using AY. Fill the centre with colonial knots using two strands of T.

Stitch five small sepals between the petals using two strands of O, working three fishbone stitches for each sepal.

INITIAL

Using O, outline the initial in back stitch. Changing to B, stitch evenly spaced French knots in the wider sections of your initial.

Forget-me-nots

Embroider tiny colonial knot forget-me-nots around the initial, using T for the centres and K for the petals.

Stitch the centre knot for each flower first. To achieve even spacing of the petals, place the first knot directly below the centre and the following two side by side above the centre knot *(diag 3)*.

diag 3

To complete the flower, place a knot in the remaining space on each side of the centre for petals 4 and 5.

Leaves

Scatter tiny detached chain stitch leaves, each with a long anchoring stitch, around the forget-me-nots using B and O.

BORDERS

Using two strands of O, embroider the borders in chain stitch, removing the tacking as you go. Whip the rows of chain stitch using two strands of B.

EMBROIDERY KEY

All embroidery is worked using one strand of thread unless otherwise specified.

Strawberry flower = K (split back stitch, padded satin stitch), AR and AY (straight stitch), T (2 strands, colonial knot)

Sepals = O (2 strands, fishbone stitch)

Initial = O (back stitch), B (French knot)

Forget-me-nots = K and T (colonial knot)

Leaves = B and O (detached chain stitch)

Borders = O (2 strands, chain stitch), B (2 strands, whipping)

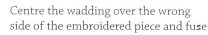

Centre the wadding over the wrong side of the embroidered piece and fuse in place, protecting your iron with a piece of baking paper.

Carefully score the interfacing along the centre from top to bottom to mark the foldline. Place it over the wadding.

Fold and press the seam allowances over the interfacing. Unfold. Fold each corner to the wrong side over the interfacing and press. Refold the seam allowances along each side to mitre the corners. Tack the seam allowances to the interfacing (*diag 1*).

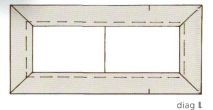

diag 1

2. Preparing and attaching the twisted cord

Cut a 70cm (27½") length of O. Knot the threads together at each end and make a twisted cord. Fold the cord in half and knot the ends together. Wrap the cord tightly before the knot with one strand of O. Take a few stitches through the wraps to secure. Don't cut the thread at this point. Undo the knot securing the cord ends and trim off the excess thread.

Stitch the wrapped end of the cord securely in place at the midpoint of the upper back seam allowance using the attached thread (*diag 2*).

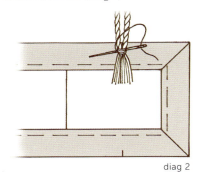

diag 2

3. Attaching the beads

Referring to the diagram, thread the beads onto a length of quilting thread (*diag 3*).

Take the thread over the last bead and pass the needle back through the beads. Tie the thread tails with a double parcel knot (left over right, left over right again, then right over left). Stitch securely in place at the midpoint of the lower back seam allowance.

diag 3

4. Making the scissor keep

Cover the curtain weight with a small piece of cotton tape. With wrong sides together and matching folded edges, fold the scissor keep along the foldline. Using matching machine sewing thread, ladder stitch the folded edges together, inserting the covered curtain weight before stitching the third side. Using three strands of O, work knotted pearl stitch over the seamline on all four edges.

Construction

The shaded areas in the following diagrams indicate the right side of the fabric.

Cutting out

Cut the pieces following the measurements below.

Lightweight fusible wadding

Cut one, 6cm x 3cm wide (2³⁄₈" x 1³⁄₁₆")

Stiff interfacing

Cut one, 6cm x 3cm wide (2³⁄₈" x 1³⁄₁₆")

Order of work

Refer to the step-by-step instructions for knotted pearl stitch on page 89.

1. Preparing the embroidered piece

Block and press the embroidered fabric following the instructions on page 37. Cut out along the marked cutting lines.

Garden spool holder

One of the oldest ways to hold spools of thread was the spool knave, an eighteenth century tool that consisted of a handle that both ends of a spool could be clipped into and hung from a chatelaine. As chatelaines are no longer commonly used, this charming thread container with a hole in the lid is an ideal accessory to help keep your embroidery thread clean and tangle free. Designed to hold a no. 8 or 12 perlé cotton ball, it features a myriad of embroidered spring blooms, garden creatures and ripe oranges.

This spool holder measures
5cm high x 5cm in diameter (2" x 2").

Requirements

Fabric

30cm (12") square of natural cotton–linen blend

10cm x 35cm wide (4" x 14") piece of pale butter and fern green print cotton

Supplies

6cm x 12mm wide (2 3/8" x 1/2") oatmeal satin ribbon

10cm x 15cm wide (4" x 6") piece of lightweight fusible interfacing

10cm x 25cm wide (4" x 10") piece of lightweight fusible wadding, e.g. Pellon

10cm x 15cm wide (4" x 6") piece of firm, medium weight wadding, e.g. Ultrafleece

10cm x 30cm wide (4" x 12") piece of template plastic

8cm x 15cm wide (3 3/16" x 6") piece of acetate

Clear nylon thread

Fine beading thread, e.g. Nymo

Quilting thread

Matching machine sewing thread

Beads & charms

1 x 6mm (1/4") green nephrite bead

17mm (11/16") brass beehive charm

2 x 7mm (5/16") brass bee charms

Equipment

See page 44.

NEEDLES

Refer to the needle chart on page 10.
No. 9 betweens
No. 8 crewel
No. 9 crewel
No. 10 crewel
No. 10 curved
No. 26 tapestry

THREADS & BEADS

Refer to the combined list of threads on page 11.
Au Papillon Fil d'Or deluxe
A
Au Ver à Soie Antique Metallics
C, D
Au Ver à Soie, Soie d'Alger
G, I
Caron Soie Cristale stranded silk
L, M, N, O
Colour Streams Silken Strands
T, U, V
DMC no. 4 soft cotton
Y
DMC stranded cotton
AA, AC, AD, AE, AF, AG, AH, AI
Gumnut Yarns 'Stars' stranded silk
AR
Madeira stranded silk
AV, AW
Weeks Dye Works stranded cotton
BE

Beads

Maria George Delica beads
BL
Non-branded craft beads
BQ

TOP

Preparation for embroidery

See the liftout pattern for the embroidery designs.

Prepare the fabric referring to the instructions on page 44. Leaving 3cm (1³/₁₆") between the pieces for the seam allowances, tack a 4.5cm x 15.2cm wide (1³/₄" x 6") rectangle for the wall and use the templates to tack the outlines for the top and base *(diag 1)*

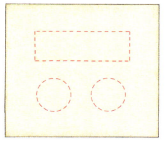

diag 1

Use the template to tack the outline for the base on the lining fabric. Aligning the tacking with the dashed outlines, transfer the embroidery designs and cutting lines following the instructions on page 9. Mark the circle for the eyelet on the lid with the water-soluble fabric marker.

Embroidery

All embroidery is worked with the fabric held taut in the hoop, using the needle in a stabbing motion.

Refer to the close-up photographs and embroidery key for colour placement.

BASE

Order of work

LID

Oranges

Stitching from the top of the fruit, cover an orange with closely worked long-armed cross stitch, using three strands of V. Gradually increase the width of the stitches for the upper half of the orange.

Smooth each stitch by placing your needle under the thread as you pull the stitch through so that the three strands lay side by side *(diag 2)*.

diag 2

From the halfway point, gradually decrease the width of the stitches to achieve a smooth round shape. Work a tiny cross stitch at the base of the orange with two strands of AG.

Leaves

See page 14 for hints on working the leaves. All the leaves are embroidered in the same manner, using two strands of G, AH or AI. Beginning at the tip, stitch an uneven fly stitch – short on one side, long on the other. For a leaf curving to the left, bring the thread to the front at (a), take it to the back at (b) and emerge at (c) to anchor the stitch *(diag 3)*.

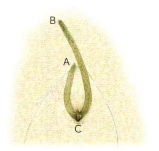

diag 3

For a leaf curving to the right, (a) should be above (b) *(diag 4)*.

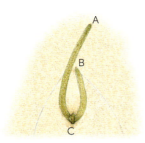

diag 4

Work fly stitches close together, gradually increasing the width of the stitches to shape the leaf. When the leaf is broad enough, gradually decrease the width of the stitches.

The anchoring stitches should line up neatly to make the mid rib of the leaf *(diag 5)*.

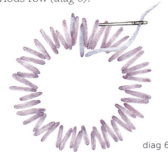

diag 5

To add gold highlights or veins, bring one strand of D to the front at the edge of the leaf, slide your needle between two adjacent stitches and take it to the back at an angle under the centre line of anchoring stitches.

Eyelet

Refer to the step-by-step instructions for working eyelets on page 86.

Using AD, work an eyelet around the marked circle.

BASE

Embroider the oranges and leaves on the base in the same manner as the lid. Embroider another orange and two leaves on the base lining fabric.

WALL

Cornflower

Using two strands of AW and starting on the outer edge of the flower, work straight stitches at differing angles, each approximately 5mm (^{3}/$_{16}$") in length. Change to I and work a second round in a similar manner, tucking the ends of the stitches under those of the previous row *(diag 6)*.

diag 6

Work a third round inside the first using two strands of AV and blending the stitches into the previous rounds. Radiating from the centre, fill the flower with seed stitch using two strands of thread and changing between AC and AF. Add straight stitch highlights using A.

Stem

Stitching from the base of the flower, embroider the stem in heavy chain stitch using two strands of AH.

Leaves

Outline the leaves in split back stitch using AR. Using the same thread, fill each leaf with long and short stitch, covering the outline.

Caterpillar

The body is padded with two lengths of soft cotton (Y), laid side by side. Leaving 1cm (^{3}/$_8$") tails of soft cotton on the back, work two long parallel stitches within the outline, ensuring the stitches are loose enough to follow the shape *(diag 7)*.

diag 7

Fold the thread tails under the caterpillar on the wrong side and whip stitch in place with U. Using the same thread, work straight stitch bars across the padding, spacing the stitches 3mm (^{1}/$_8$") apart.

Change to the fine tapestry needle and, starting on the underside of the caterpillar, work rows of raised stem stitch along the body. Stop and start each row on the marked outline to create a rounded head and tail. Once all the bars are filled, couch across the caterpillar with O. Angle the couching stitches under the body and pull firmly to create little fat segments.

Embroider the legs with tiny pairs of straight stitches using C, and work two longer straight stitches into the same hole at the top for each horn *(diag 8)*.

WALL

diag 8

Attach two beads (BL) for the eyes with the fine beading thread. Place a stitch over the thread between the beads to pull them into place (diag 9).

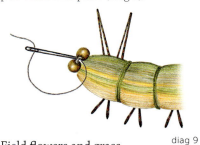

diag 9

Field flowers and grass

Refer to the step-by-step instructions for raised cross stitch on page 95.

Grass

Using two strands of AH or BE, work straight stitches of differing lengths and angles 5mm ($^3/_{16}$") from the lower tacked line. To lessen the risk of puckering and decrease the amount of thread on the back, work the stitches as shown (diag 10).

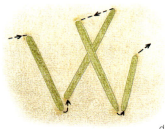

diag 10

Wheat

Using two strands of T, work the wheat in feather stitch.

Dill weed

To embroider the dill weed, work the stems in stem stitch and fly stitch with BE. Embroider the flower head with five to seven pistil stitches of varying lengths, fanning out from the top of the stem.

Pink anemones

Referring to the close-up photographs for colour placement, work a raised cross stitch at the position of each flower, using two strands of L, M or N. Work a colonial knot at the centre of each flower using two strands of AA.

Cream daisies

Stitch three detached chains for the petals, with two strands of AE, working the centre stitch first. Change to V and work a colonial knot for the flower centre.

Blue forget-me-nots

Using two strands of I, stitch a granitos for each petal. For each granitos work three stitches into the same holes. Leave a tiny space in the centre (diag 11).

diag 11

Change to two strands of V and work a colonial knot for the flower centre.

Using I, stitch pairs of colonial knots among the flowers for the tiny buds.

Beads and charms

Using the clear nylon thread, attach the beehive to the left of the cornflower and the two bees on either side above the flower. Attach three blue flower beads (BQ) above the caterpillar using matching machine sewing thread.

EMBROIDERY KEY

All embroidery is worked with one strand of thread unless otherwise specified.

Lid and base

Oranges = V (3 strands, long-armed cross stitch), AG (2 strands, cross stitch)

Leaves = G, AH or AI (2 strands, fly stitch), D (straight stitch)

Eyelet = AD (running stitch, back stitch, overcast stitch)

Wall

Cornflower = I, AV and AW (2 strands, straight stitch), AC and AF (2 strands, seed stitch), A (straight stitch)

Stem = AH (2 strands, heavy chain stitch)

Leaves = AR (split back stitch, long and short stitch)

Caterpillar = Y (straight stitch), U (straight stitch, raised stem stitch), O (couching)

Legs and horns = C (straight stitch)

Eyes = BL (beading)

Field flowers and grass

Grass = AH or BE (2 strands, straight stitch)

Wheat = T (2 strands, feather stitch)

Dill weed = BE (stem stitch, fly stitch, pistil stitch)

Pink anemone = L, M or N (2 strands, raised cross stitch), AA (2 strands, colonial knot)

Cream daisies = AE (2 strands, detached chain), V (2 strands, colonial knot)

Blue forget-me-nots = I (2 strands, granitos, 3 stitches), V (2 strands, colonial knot)

Tiny buds = I (2 strands, colonial knot)

Construction

The shaded areas in the following diagrams indicate the right side of the fabric.

Cutting out

See the liftout pattern for the templates.

Where templates are not provided, cut the pieces following the measurements below.

Template plastic

Wall: cut one, 16.5cm x 4.2cm wide (6½" x 1¹¹/₁₆")

Lightweight fusible wadding

Wall: cut one, 16.5cm x 4.2cm wide (6½" x 1⅞")

Order of work

Refer to the step-by-step instructions for working eyelets on page 86, knotted pearl stitch on page 89 and up and down blanket stitch loop on page 99.

1. Preparing the embroidered pieces

Block the embroidery following the instructions on page 37. Cut out each piece along the marked cutting lines.

2. Constructing the wall and lining

Fuse the corresponding lightweight wadding piece to the wrong side of the embroidered wall piece, making sure it is centred.

With right sides together and matching raw edges, pin the wall lining and embroidered piece together along the lower edge. Machine stitch the seam and trim the seam allowance to 5mm (³/₁₆"). Press the seam allowance towards the embroidered wall.

With right sides together and matching the seam and edges, fold the piece in half across the width. Beginning on the embroidered piece, stitch the centre back seam, tapering the seam so that it is 3mm (⅛") wider on the lining (*diag 1*).

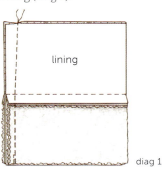

lining

diag 1

Press the seam open. Embroider three pink anemones with stems and grass over the centre back seam on the embroidered panel, referring to the instructions on page 65.

Turn under the seam allowance of the remaining long edge of the lining fabric and tack in place (*diag 2*).

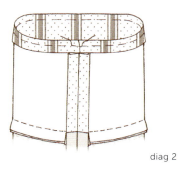

diag 2

Fold the embroidered piece over the lining. Overlap the short ends of the template plastic wall piece by 6mm (¼") and secure with double sided tape, bringing the tape over the edges of the plastic (*diag 3*).

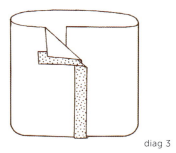

diag 3

Secure with a piece of single-sided sticky tape over the join again.

Insert the plastic tube between the embroidered wall piece and the lining. Fold the seam allowance of the embroidered piece over the plastic and behind the lining (*diag 4*).

diag 4

Use the curved needle and matching machine sewing thread to ladder stitch the lining to the embroidered wall along the upper edge.

3. Making the top

Use the awl to punch a hole in the centre of the template plastic top circle. Push a hole in the centre of each wadding piece in the same manner. Use the tips of your scissors to enlarge the holes in each. Apply a small amount of glue to the plastic top piece and, with the fusible side facing up, glue the smaller piece of lightweight wadding in place, aligning the holes in each (*diag 5*).

diag 5

Centre the medium weight wadding over the lightweight wadding, aligning the holes, and fuse in place, protecting your iron with a piece of baking paper.

Fuse a larger circle of lightweight wadding to the wrong side of the embroidered piece, after making and enlarging a hole in the centre of the wadding as before.

With the padded side facing down and aligning the holes, place the prepared plastic circle on the wrong side of the embroidered piece. Using the quilting thread, work a row of gathering stitch around the embroidered piece 1cm (3/8") from the seam line. Pull the thread, gathering the seam allowance to the wrong side. Lace the seam allowance over the plastic, avoiding the eyelet (*diag 6*).

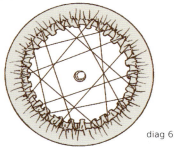

diag 6

Lining

Fuse the interfacing to the wrong side of the unembroidered lining piece. With one strand of matching stranded cotton, work an eyelet in the centre. Press gently (*diag 7*).

diag 7

Work a row of gathering stitch around the edge in the same manner as before. Punch a hole in the centre of one of the acetate circles. Aligning the holes, place the acetate circle on the wrong side of the lining and pull up the gathering thread tightly. Secure with a couple of back stitches (*diag 8*).

diag 8

With wrong sides together and aligning the centre holes, ladder stitch the lining to the spool holder top.

Pin the top of the spool holder into position on the top of the embroidered wall, ensuring the grain is aligned with the centre back seam (*diag 9*).

diag 9

Ladder stitch the upper edge of the wall to the embroidered top from the outside, using matching machine sewing thread in the curved needle.

Starting near the centre back seam, embroider knotted pearl stitch around the edge of the top using three strands of O.

4. Making the base and base lining

With the fusible side facing up, glue the remaining small lightweight wadding circle to the template plastic base piece in the same manner as before. Centre the medium wadding over the lightweight wadding and fuse in place as before.

Prepare the cover and lining for the base in the same manner as the top, omitting the eyelet, but do not stitch together at this stage. When preparing the embroidered cover, make sure the embroidery is centred before lacing in a clockwise direction.

5. Making and attaching the hinge and base lining

Fold the satin ribbon in half across the width and finger press the fold. Unfold. Centre the foldline over the seam on the lower edge of the centre back wall. Stitch in place with small back stitches along the foldline at the lower edge of the wall piece (*diag 10*).

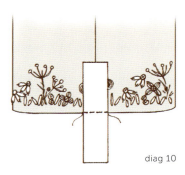

diag 10

Refold the ribbon and position on the wrong side of the prepared base cover. Make sure it is facing the right way, so the embroidery will be outermost when the base is closed. Stitch securely to the seam allowance on the base (*diag 11*).

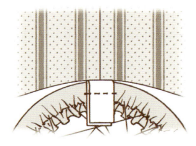

diag 11

With wrong sides together, ladder stitch the lining to the base.

Work knotted pearl stitch with three strands of O around the edge of the base.

Attach the nephrite bead at the centre front of the lower wall edge and work an up and down blanket stitch loop to correspond on the edge of the base.

Strawberry tape measure cover

Replacing traditional measuring sticks, tape measures emerged in the eighteenth century and were usually fabric ribbons – often silk – housed in cylindrical metal containers with small handles to rewind the tape. Today's tape measures are often retracted by pressing a button on the side. This exquisite cover makes a pretty home for your tape measure, while still allowing you to press the button and retract the tape. Stitched onto natural linen, a tiny brass honey bee enticed by the fragrance of luscious ripening berries hovers on the front, while a single delicate strawberry blossom decorates the back.

The cover measures 5.5cm (2 1/4") in diameter.

Requirements

Fabric

30cm (12") square of natural cotton–linen blend

Supplies

5cm (2") square of 14-count waste canvas

7cm x 15cm wide (2 3/4" x 6") piece of lightweight fusible wadding, e.g. Pellon

3cm x 20cm wide (1 1/4" x 8") piece of lightweight non-fusible wadding, e.g. Pellon

6cm x 15cm wide (2 3/8" x 6") piece of firm, medium weight wadding, e.g. Ultrafleece

6cm x 15cm wide (2 3/8" x 6") piece of template plastic

3cm x 20cm wide (1 1/4" x 8") piece of acetate

Soft beading wire, e.g. Tigertail

Quilting thread

Matching machine sewing thread

Beads & charms

8mm (5/16") green lamp bead with pink flowers

8mm (5/16") gold saucer bead

6mm (1/4") unakite bead

4mm (3/16") green frosted bead

4mm (3/16") brass spacer bead

4 x 2mm (1/16") round gold beads

gold crimp bead

Susan Clarke Originals

Bee – 201

Equipment

See page 44.

Refer to the needle chart on page 10.

No. 9 betweens
No. 8 crewel
No. 9 crewel
No. 10 crewel
No. 26 tapestry

THREADS

Refer to the combined list of threads on page 11.

Au Papillon Fil d'Or deluxe
A, B

Au Ver à Soie Antique Metallics
C, D

Au Ver à Soie, Soie d'Alger
G, K

Caron Soie Cristale stranded silk
O

Caron Wildflowers perlé cotton
R

Colour Streams Silken Strands
T, U

DMC stranded cotton
AD

Gumnut Yarns 'Stars' stranded silk
AR, AS

Rajmahal stranded rayon
AY

The Gentle Art Sampler Threads
BA

Preparation for embroidery

See the liftout pattern for the embroidery designs.

Prepare the fabric referring to the instructions on page 44.

Aligning the tacking with the dashed outlines, transfer the embroidery designs and cutting lines following the instructions on page 9.

Embroidery

All embroidery is worked with the fabric held taut in the hoop, using the needle in a stabbing motion. Refer to the close-up photographs and embroidery key for colour placement.

Order of work

STRAWBERRY

Refer to the step-by-step instructions for knotted pearl stitch on page 89, needlewoven picot on page 91 and Rococo stitch variation on page 95.

Outline the strawberry in split back stitch using BA. Tack the square of waste canvas over the strawberry outline, carefully aligning it with the grain of the fabric (diag 1).

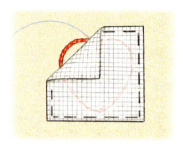

diag 1

Using BA and beginning at the centre top of the berry, work a row of Rococo stitch variation across the upper edge of the shape, keeping the couching stitches aligned. To achieve a smooth rounded shape, work the outermost stitches a little loose to elongate each lozenge shape on one side (diag 2).

diag 2

Embroider the second row in a similar manner, interlocking the stitches into the first row. Continue to work rows to fill the shape, adjusting the stitches at the sides to achieve a smooth edge. Carefully withdraw the canvas threads with the eye of a needle.

Seeds

To embroider the seeds, scatter French knots across the berry using two strands of A. Take care not to pull the stitches too tight, so the knots sit on top of the previous stitching.

Sepals

Using two strands of O, work three needlewoven picots at the top of the berry for the sepals.

Stem

Embroider the stem in knotted pearl stitch with three strands of AS. Begin at the base of the stem and slide the needle under the picots as you near the top of the berry.

Work the small scroll at the top of the stem in coral stitch with two strands of the same thread.

UNRIPE BERRY

Stem

Embroider the stem in chain stitch using two strands of AS. Whip the stitches using the same thread.

Berry

Working from the edge of the berry towards the centre, fill the unripe berry with closely packed colonial knots using R. Use each section of the thread to create patches of colour.

Sepals

Using two strands of O, stitch a large detached chain for each sepal. Change to one strand of B and add a long straight stitch over each anchoring stitch for highlights (diag 3).

diag 3

LARGE LEAF

Outline the leaf with small split back stitches using AR. Embroider the outer edge of the leaf in long and short stitch with the same thread, working each stitch from inside the shape and over the outline. Gradually change the angle of the stitches to follow the direction of the veins.

Thread one strand each of G and O into separate needles and work the second row of long and short stitch, splitting the end of the stitches in the previous row and changing between the two needles. The greater the difference between the tones of green, the more staggered the boundary should be. Always leave the spare thread on top of your work, so it will not get caught on the back.

Leave a narrow space along the centre of the leaf for the vein. Stitching from the base towards the tip, work the centre vein in stem stitch with U. Embroider long straight stitches for the side veins using the same thread. Change to D and work straight stitch highlights along the veins.

CATERPILLAR

Using three strands of AR, work a 30 wrap bullion knot. Shape and couch the knot in place with a few couching stitches, using one strand of the same thread. Work a colonial knot for the head. Changing to C, work a few tiny straight stitches for the legs.

STRAWBERRY FLOWER

Outline the petals in split back stitch using one strand of K, stitching a single row between the petals and around the flower centre (diag 4).

diag 4

Using the same thread, work two layers of satin stitch padding, ensuring the uppermost layer is worked across the width of the petals. Embroider satin stitch over the padding, bringing the thread to the front on the outer edge and taking the needle to the back over the outline on the inner edge. If your stitches become too crowded, work some ¾ length stitches. Changing to AR, work a straight stitch to mark the divisions of the petals.

Embroider three straight stitches of varying lengths over each petal using AY. Fill the centre with colonial knots using two strands of T.

Stitch five small sepals between the petals using two strands of O, working three fishbone stitches for each sepal.

EMBROIDERY KEY

All embroidery is worked using one strand of thread unless otherwise specified.

Strawberry

Berry = BA (2 strands, Rococo stitch variation)

Seeds = A (2 strands, French knot)

Sepals = O
(2 strands, needlewoven picot)

Stem = AS (3 strands, knotted pearl stitch, 2 strands, coral stitch)

Unripe berry

Stalk = AS (2 strands, chain stitch, whipping)

Berry = R (colonial knot)

Sepals = O (2 strands, detached chain stitch), B (straight stitch)

Leaf = AR (split back stitch, long and short stitch), O and G (long and short stitch), U (stem stitch, straight stitch), D (straight stitch)

Caterpillar

Body = AR (3 strands, bullion knot, 30 wraps, 1 strand, couching)

Head = AR (colonial knot)

Legs = C (straight stitch)

Strawberry flower

Flower = K (split back stitch, padded satin stitch), AR and AY (straight stitch), T (2 strands, colonial knot)

Sepals = O (2 strands, fishbone stitch)

FRONT

BACK

Strawberries are the angels of the earth, innocent and sweet with green leafy wings reaching heavenward.

Terri Guillemets

Construction

The shaded areas in the following diagrams indicate the right side of the fabric.

Cutting out

See the liftout pattern for templates.

Where templates are not provided, cut the pieces following the measurements given below.

Cotton–linen blend

Wall: cut one, 3.7cm x 18.6cm wide (1 $\frac{7}{16}$" x 7 $\frac{5}{16}$")

Lightweight non-fusible wadding

Wall: cut one, 1.7cm x 16.5cm wide ($\frac{11}{16}$" x 6 $\frac{1}{2}$")

Acetate

Wall: cut one, 1.7cm x 16.6cm wide ($\frac{11}{16}$" x 6 $\frac{9}{16}$")

Order of work

Refer to the step-by-step instructions for lacing and mitring fabric over mountboard on page 88 and knotted pearl stitch on page 89.

1. Preparing the embroidered piece

Block the embroidery following the instructions on page 37. Cut out each piece along the marked cutting line.

2. Making the front and back

Apply a small amount of glue to one side of each template plastic piece. Place a circle of medium weight wadding on each piece and leave to dry.

Gently fuse a lightweight fusible wadding piece to the wrong side of the embroidered front and back pieces.

Using quilting thread, work a row of gathering stitches around the edge of each embroidered piece.

With the padded side facing down, place a padded plastic circle on the wrong side of one embroidered piece. Pull up the gathering thread, gathering the seam allowance to the wrong side. Lace the seam allowance over the plastic (*diag 1*).

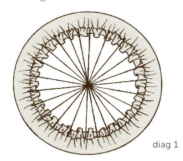

diag 1

Repeat for the remaining piece.

3. Making the wall

Work a row of machine zigzag along each long edge of the wall piece.

Glue the piece of wadding to the acetate strip with a small amount of glue and allow to dry. With the wadding facing down, centre the acetate strip over the wrong side of the fabric piece.

Lace and mitre the fabric over the padded acetate (*diag 2*).

diag 2

4. Attaching the wall

Starting at the right hand quarter mark, ladder stitch the edge of the wall to the back circle using the curved needle. Leave a 6mm (¼") gap between the ends of the wall to allow the tape measure to retract easily.

Ensuring correct orientation, ladder stitch the front cover to the remaining wall edge, stopping at the halfway point to insert the tape measure. Make sure the tag of the tape measure is protruding out of the opening.

Using three strands of O, work knotted pearl stitch over the seamlines at the top and bottom.

5. Finishing

Cut a 15cm (6") length of soft beading wire. Starting with the crimp and referring to the diagram, thread the larger beads onto the wire, finishing with two small gold beads (*diag 3*).

Pass the wire through the folded end of the metal tag of the tape measure and thread the two remaining small round gold beads. Pass the wire back down through the beads (*diag 4*).

diag 3   diag 4

Adjust the beads so that they are even around the metal tag. Push the crimp hard against the lowest bead and clamp it tight around the wires using a pair of long nosed pliers.

Trim the excess wire.

Heartsease thimble holder

Whether highly ornate or humble and practical, the thimble is one of the most widely used needlework tools. It can be fashioned from metal, wood, leather, china or glass, and embellished with filigree work or precious gems. Ornamented with a delicate embroidered heartsease and textured surface stitchery, this meticulously fashioned thimble holder will make a perfect home for your everyday thimble.

The thimble holder measures 3.5cm high x 3cm in diameter (1 3/8" x 1 3/16").

Requirements

Fabric

30cm (12") square of natural cotton–linen blend

5cm x 15cm wide (2" x 6") piece of silk broadcloth

Supplies

5cm x 15cm wide (2" x 6") piece of lightweight non-fusible wadding, e.g. Pellon

5cm x 15cm wide (2" x 6") piece of lightweight fusible wadding, e.g. Pellon

5cm (2") square of firm, medium weight wadding, e.g. Ultrafleece

5cm x 10cm wide (2" x 4") piece of template plastic

3cm (1 1/4") square of acetate

Quilting thread

Matching machine sewing thread

Beads

1 x 6mm (1/4") green nephrite bead

Equipment

See page 44.

NEEDLES

Refer to the needle chart on page 10.

No. 9 betweens
No. 8 crewel
No. 9 crewel
No. 10 crewel
No. 10 curved
No. 26 tapestry

THREADS & BEADS

Refer to the combined list of threads on page 11.

Au Ver à Soie Antique Metallics
D

Au Ver à Soie, Soie d'Alger
E, F, J

Caron Soie Cristale stranded silk
O, P

Colour Streams Silken Strands
T

DMC stranded cotton
A E

Scansilk 100% rayon machine thread
A Z

Preparation for embroidery

See the liftout pattern for the embroidery designs and template pieces.

Prepare the fabric referring to the instructions on page 44. Aligning the tacking with the dashed outlines, transfer the embroidery designs and cutting lines following the instructions on page 9, using the water-soluble marker for the stripes on the wall piece. Cut one lining piece from the silk broadcloth, referring to the template on the liftout pattern.

Embroidery

All embroidery is worked with the fabric held taut in the hoop, using the needle in a stabbing motion.

Refer to the close-up photographs and embroidery key for colour placement.

Order of work

WALL

The wall is embroidered with a repeat design of four different stripes.

Row 1

Using two strands of O, embroider rows of coral stitch along the marked lines, keeping the knots close together (*diag 1*).

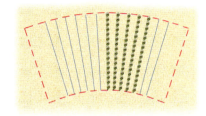

diag 1

When all the coral stitch rows are completed, carefully remove the blue pen with a moist cotton bud. Fold your embroidery in a towel and gently press to remove any excess moisture. Dry the piece quickly.

Row 2

Work a row of stem stitch along the right hand side of each coral stitch row using D.

Row 3

Embroider a row of stem stitch with F to the left of each coral stitch row.

Row 4

Using two strands of O, work a row of running stitch to the left of each stem stitch row, keeping the stitch length longer on top of your work than behind (*diag 2*).

diag 2

Change to two strands of P in the fine tapestry needle and whip the running stitches. Whip in the opposite direction with one strand of D (*diag 3*).

diag 3

BASE

Outline the dashed circle in split back stitch with O. Using two strands of the same thread, work a layer of satin stitch padding inside the outline. Start along the centre and fill one half at a time, taking the needle to the back and emerging on the same side of the circle so that there are no long stitches on the back of your work (*diag 4*).

diag 4

Still using two strands of the same thread, work satin stitch over the padding and the outline in a similar manner, placing the stitches in the opposite direction to the padding stitches. Take the needle through the fabric at an angle so that your stitches hug the outline (*diag 5*).

diag 5

Using two strands of P, place seven long stitches 2mm (1/16") apart at right angles to the satin stitches across the circle. Work a second layer of seven stitches in the opposite direction to form a lattice.

Changing to D, place a long stitch along the right hand side of each of the previous lattice stitches (diag 6).

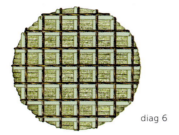

diag 6

Couch each intersection of the lattice in place with a small straight stitch over both threads using F.

LID

Heartsease

Referring to the diagram, outline petals one and two in split back stitch using E. Outline petals three and four using J and petal five using F in the same manner (diag 7).

diag 7

Using the same threads, work one layer of padding within the outlines of petals one, three and four. Work two layers of padding within the outlines of the remaining two petals, ensuring the uppermost layer is worked across each shape.

Cover the petals with satin stitch, angling the stitches towards the centre of the flower. To avoid bulk, work some stitches a little shorter, tucking them under the previous stitches to achieve a smooth finish. Add three straight stitch highlights on petals three and four, and five stitches on petal five using AZ.

Stitch a colonial knot for the flower centre with two strands of T. Using AE, work two straight stitches shaped as an upside-down 'V' above the knot.

Place a second pair of stitches on top of the first. Change to P and work a fly stitch with a small anchoring stitch below the knot (diag 8).

diag 8

Embroider the four sepals in fishbone stitch using two strands of O, stitching each from the tip towards the petals.

Lid lining

Work three colonial knot forget-me-nots at the centre of the cream silk piece, referring to the instructions on page 33. Use two strands of T for the centres and two strands of E for the petals. Work three pairs of tiny detached chain leaves with one strand of P.

EMBROIDERY KEY

All embroidery is worked using one strand of thread unless otherwise specified.

Wall

Row 1 = O (2 strands, coral stitch)

Row 2 = D (stem stitch)

Row 3 = F (stem stitch)

Row 4 = O (2 strands, running stitch), P (2 strands, whipping), D (whipping)

Base = O (split back stitch, 2 strands, padded satin stitch), P (2 strands, straight stitch), D (straight stitch), F (couching)

Lid

Heartsease = E, F or J (split back stitch, padded satin stitch, satin stitch), AZ (straight stitch)

Centre = T (2 strands, colonial knot), AE (straight stitch), P (fly stitch)

Sepals = O (2 strands, fishbone stitch)

Lid lining

Forget-me-nots = E and T (2 strands, colonial knot)

Leaves = P (detached chain stitch)

Construction

The shaded areas in the following diagrams indicate the right side of the fabric.

Cutting out

See the liftout pattern for the templates.

Order of work

Refer to the step-by-step instructions for lacing and mitring fabric over mountboard on page 88, knotted pearl stitch on page 89 and up and down blanket stitch loop on page 99.

1. Preparing the embroidered pieces

Block and press the embroidered fabric following the instructions on page 37. Cut out each piece along the marked cutting line.

2. Constructing the wall

With right sides together and matching raw edges, machine stitch the centre back seam of the emboidered piece. Finger press the seam open and turn to the right side.

Overlap the short ends of the template plastic piece by 4mm (³/₁₆") and secure with double sided tape, bringing the tape over the edges of the plastic (diag 1).

diag 1

Secure with a piece of normal tape over the join again. Apply a small amount of glue to the outside edge of the plastic. Leave until the glue is tacky, and then glue the wadding in place around the wall (diag 2).

diag 2

Slide the embroidered wall over the padded plastic and fold the upper and lower edges to the inside. Using the quilting thread, lace the edges over the plastic, ensuring the fabric is smooth and the stripes are straight.

3. Constructing and attaching the base

Apply tiny dabs of glue to the plastic base piece and glue the smaller wadding circle in place. Protecting your iron and ironing board with baking paper, fuse the larger wadding to the wrong side of the embroidered base piece, ensuring it is perfectly centred over the embroidery. Using the quilting thread, work a row of gathering stitch around the base piece, 2mm (1/8") from the raw edge *(diag 3)*.

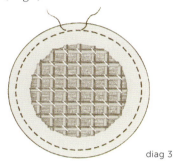

diag 3

With the padded sides together, position the plastic base over the wrong side of the embroidered base. Pull the gathering thread firmly to gather the seam allowance over the plastic, and secure. Lace the seam allowance in an anticlockwise direction *(diag 4)*.

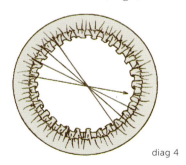

diag 4

Ladder stitch the lower edge of the wall to the embroidered base.

4. Making and attaching the lining

With right sides together and matching raw edges, overcast stitch the centre back seam of the wall lining. Finger press the seam to one side. Clip the

curves and finger press the upper and lower raw edges under. Tack in place.

Work a row of tiny back stitches along the stitchline of the base lining. Measure and mark quarter points along the lower edge of the wall and the stitchline of the base. Matching quarter marks, position the folded lower edge of the wall lining to align with the backstitching on the base lining and secure with a small stitch at the quarter points *(diag 5)*.

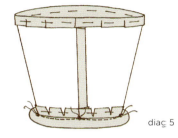

diag 5

Working from the wrong side, overcast stitch the base to the wall, catching the fold of the wall to the back stitches of the base *(diag 6)*.

diag 6

Insert the lining into the thimble holder with a thimble on your finger to push it down. Overcast stitch the upper edges of the lining and embroidered wall together.

5. Constructing and attaching the lid

With the glue side facing up, glue the small wadding piece to the template plastic lid piece. Centre the medium weight wadding over the small wadding piece and fuse in place. Centre the larger fusible wadding piece over the wrong side of the embroidered lid piece and fuse in place. Using the quilting thread, work a row of gathering stitch around the lid piece, 2mm (1/8") from the raw edge.

With the padded sides together, position the plastic lid over the wrong side of the embroidered piece, ensuring the heartsease is centred. Pull the gathering thread and lace the seam allowance over the plastic in the same manner as the base.

6. Constructing and attaching the lid lining

Glue the wadding to the acetate. Work a row of gathering stitch around the edge of the silk lining. Gather and lace the seam allowance over the padded acetate in a similar manner to the base.

With wrong sides together, centre the silk lining on the lid and ladder stitch in place.

Starting near the centre back seam, embroider knotted pearl stitch around the edge of the lid using three strands of O. As you reach the starting point, incorporate the upper edge of the wall at the centre back seam in the stitching to attach the lid *(diag 7)*.

diag 7

Using matching machine sewing thread, attach the 6mm (1/4") bead at the centre front of the wall, 4mm (3/16") below the upper edge.

Work an up and down blanket stitch loop at the centre front of the lid using three strands of O. Remove all visible tacking stitches.

Beaded thread counter

This tool is invaluable for counting threads on linen and other counted fabrics. Simply place one needle at your starting point, then count the required number of threads and insert the second needle. Gleaming metallic threads and richly ornamented beads embellish the gorgeous tassel and fine twisted cords adorning this thread counter. Many thanks to Janet Luce for loaning me her thread counter for reference.

The thread counter measures 19.5cm (7 $^{11}/_{16}$") in length.

Requirements

Supplies
4cm x 8cm wide (1 $^3/_{16}$" x 3 $^3/_{16}$") piece of card, e.g. cereal packet
2 x no. 28 tapestry needles

Beads
8mm ($^5/_{16}$") green lamp bead with pink flower
6mm ($^1/_4$") nephrite bead
8mm ($^5/_{16}$") gold saucer bead
4mm ($^3/_{16}$") green frosted glass bead
4mm ($^3/_{16}$") gold spacer bead
3 x 2mm ($^1/_{16}$") round gold beads

Equipment
See page 44.

NEEDLE
No. 26 tapestry needle

THREADS
Refer to the combined list of threads on page 11.
Au Papillon Fil d'Or deluxe
A
YLI silk floss
BG (1 pkt)

Order of work
Making the twisted cords
Cut two 50cm (19 $^3/_4$") lengths and two 30cm (12") lengths of BG.

Thread one no. 28 tapestry needle onto one 50cm (19 $^3/_4$") length of thread. Knot each end of the thread and make a twisted cord, sliding the needle to the middle before you fold the twisted thread in half and allow it to twist back on itself. Knot the ends together. Repeat for the remaining no. 28 needle and long thread.

Knot the cords together 13.5cm (5 $^5/_{16}$") below the needles (*diag 1*).

diag 1

Making the tassel
Score the piece of card and fold in half, forming a 4cm (1 $^1/_2$") square. Starting at the cut edges, wind the remaining silk thread around the folded card.

Place the wrapped threads neatly side by side and avoid overlapping.

Thread a 30cm (12") length of BG in the tapestry needle. Moisten the thread thoroughly and slide under the wrapped threads at the folded end of the card.

Slide sharp scissors between the open ends of the card and carefully cut the threads. Open out the card, trying not to disturb the cut threads. Lay the knot of the twisted cords on top of the cut threads just below the foldline (diag 2).

diag 2

Tie the moist thread in a double parcel knot, left over right, left over right again, then right over left, just above the knot in the cords. Carefully wrap the threads around the cord (diag 3).

diag 3

Knot again. Carefully smooth the threads down over the knot in the cords to form the tassel skirt.

Thread up the remaining 30cm (12") length of thread and moisten it thoroughly as before. Placing the tail at the lower edge of the skirt, wrap the threads securely three times, just below the knot in the cords for the neck (diag 4).

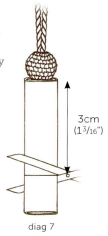

diag 4

Secure the thread by working a couple of blanket stitches around the wraps. Pass the needle down through the skirt and trim the thread level with the skirt. Wrap the skirt in cling wrap to protect it.

Needlelace tassel head

Cut a 1m (40") length of one strand of A. Thread into the tapestry needle and knot the tail. Slide the needle down through the head of the tassel, emerging just below the wraps and pulling the knot into the tassel head. Work detached blanket stitches around the threads wrapping the neck, spacing the stitches a needle width apart (diag 5).

diag 5

When reaching the starting point, work a second round of detached blanket stitch, placing a stitch into each stitch of the previous row. Continue to cover the tassel head with detached blanket stitch in this manner, slightly increasing the stitch length as the head widens and decreasing as it becomes smaller at the top. To finish, pass the needle backwards and forwards very carefully through the head of the tassel. Pull the thread taut and trim the tail, allowing it to spring back into the head.

Thread up three strands of A and wrap the neck to cover the green silk wraps, starting the thread as before. Secure with two blanket stitches around the wraps and thread the tail into the head to finish.

Neatening the skirt

Remove the cling wrap. Trim the knots of the twisted cords level with the skirt (diag 6).

Use an eyebrow comb to smooth the skirt. Slightly dampened hands also help.

On the lightweight paper, draw a line 3cm (1³/₁₆") from one edge. Wrap the tassel skirt tightly in the paper so that the edge of the paper is at the neck of the tassel. Cut through the paper and skirt on the pencil line with one cut using very sharp dressmaker's scissors (diag 7).

Thread both needles of the thread counter through the beads, referring to the close-up photograph for the order of the beads. Slide the beads down the cords so that the first bead is hard against the head of the tassel.

Knot the cords together above the last bead, using a needle to position the knot closely against the bead.

diag 6

diag 7

3cm (1³/₁₆")

Beehive thread cutter cover

Traditionally scissors have been the tool of choice for cutting embroidery threads, but with increasing security concerns, travelling stitchers have turned to circular thread cutters as the perfect solution. Adorned with tiny pink anemones, blue forget-me-nots and cheerful daisies surrounding a honey beehive, this delightful cover not only makes your thread cutter easy to find, it can also double as a pretty pendant.

The cover measures 5.3cm x 5.3cm wide (2 1/8" x 2 1/8").

Requirements

Fabric

20cm (8") square of natural cotton–linen blend

10cm x 20cm wide (4" x 8") piece of pale butter and fern green print cotton

5cm x 10cm wide (2" x 4") piece of brown wool felt

Supplies

10cm x 20cm wide (4" x 8") piece lightweight fusible wadding, e.g. Pellon

10cm x 20cm wide (4" x 8") piece of firm, medium weight wadding, e.g. Ultrafleece

10cm x 20cm wide (4" x 8") piece of lightweight fusible interfacing

5cm x 10cm wide (2" x 4") piece of appliqué paper

10cm x 20cm wide (4" x 8") piece of template plastic

3cm (1 1/4") diameter thread cutter, e.g. Clover

Quilting thread

Matching machine sewing thread

Beads

2 x 8mm (5/16") green lamp beads with pink flowers

4 x 4mm (3/16") antique gold spacer beads

Equipment

See page 44.

NEEDLES

Refer to the needle chart on page 10.

No. 5 crewel
No. 9 crewel
No. 10 crewel
No. 10 curved
No. 26 tapestry

THREADS & BEADS

Au Ver à Soie, Soie d'Alger
I

Caron Soie Cristale stranded silk
L, M, O

Colour Streams Silken Strands
T, V

DMC no. 8 perlé cotton
X

DMC stranded cotton
AA, AE, AH

Gumnut Yarns 'Daisies' fine wool
AP

Weeks Dye Works
BE

YLI fine metallic
BK

Beads

Mill Hill petite seed beads
BP

Non-branded craft beads
BQ

Preparation for embroidery

See the liftout pattern for the embroidery designs.

Prepare the cotton–linen referring to the instructions on page 44. Aligning the tacking with the dashed outlines, transfer the embroidery designs and cutting lines following the instructions on page 9.

Embroidery

See the liftout pattern for the beehive templates.

All embroidery is worked with the fabric held taut in the hoop, using the needle in a stabbing motion.

Refer to the close-up photographs and embroidery key for colour placement.

Order of work

BEEHIVE

Refer to the step-by-step instructions for Portuguese knotted stem stitch on page 94.

Using the pencil, trace the three hive templates onto appliqué paper. Fuse the paper onto the brown felt. Cut out along the marked lines and remove the paper backing. With the adhesive side facing down, centre the smallest piece at the position for the hive, above

the hive opening, and stab stitch in place with matching thread. Place the medium shape on top and secure in the same manner. Position the largest piece on top and work a stab stitch at the centre top and each corner to ensure the beehive is straight before working stab stitch around the shape *(diag 1)*.

diag 1

Using two strands of AP, work nine vertical foundation stitches across the padding, starting at the centre and stitching towards one side at a time *(diag 2)*.

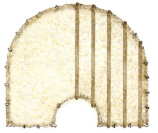

diag 2

Working from the base of the beehive, cover the felt padding with woven filling stitch. Make sure to work two rows for each weaving sequence. Stitching from the centre towards one side at a time, fill the opening with vertical satin stitches using AA.

Embroider the base of the beehive in Portuguese knotted stem stitch using two strands of AP.

Work the handle at the top of the hive in whipped chain stitch using one strand of the same thread.

BEES

Using two strands of AA, work a colonial knot at the centre of each bee on both the front and back pieces. Change to two strands of T and work a colonial knot on each side of the black knot for the body. Stitch a tiny detached chain for each wing using BK *(diag 3)*.

diag 3

FIELD FLOWERS AND GRASS

Refer to the step-by-step instructions for raised cross stitch on page 95.

Grass

Using two strands of AH or BE work straight stitches of differing lengths and angles 5mm (³⁄₁₆") from the lower tacked line. To lessen the risk of puckering and decrease the amount of thread on the back, work the stitches as shown (*diag 4*).

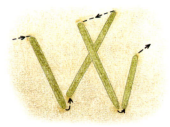

diag 4

Dill weed

To embroider the dill weed, work the stems in stem stitch and fly stitch with BE. Embroider the flower head with five to seven pistil stitches of varying lengths, fanning out from the top of the stem.

Pink anemones

Referring to the close-up photographs for colour placement, work a raised cross stitch at the position of each flower, using two strands of L or M. Work a colonial knot at the centre of each flower using two strands of AA.

Cream daisies

Stitch three detached chains for the petals, with two strands of AE, working the centre stitch first. Change to V and work a colonial knot for the flower centre.

Blue forget-me-nots

Using two strands of I, stitch a granitos for each petal. For each granitos work three stitches into the same holes. Leave a tiny space in the centre (*diag 5*).

diag 5

Change to two strands of V and work a colonial knot for the flower centre.

Beads

Attach three blue flower beads (BQ) among the flowers on the back piece using matching machine sewing thread.

EMBROIDERY KEY

Beehive = AP (2 strands, woven filling stitch, Portuguese knotted stem stitch, 1 strand, chain stitch, whipping), AA (satin stitch)

Bees = T and AA (2 strands, colonial knot), BK (detached chain stitch)

Field flowers and grass

Grass = AH or BE
(2 strands, straight stitch)

Dill weed = BE
(straight stitch, pistil stitch)

Pink anemones = L or M (2 strands, raised cross stitch), AA (2 strands, colonial knot)

Cream daisies = AE (2 strands, detached chain stitch), V (2 strands, colonial knot)

Blue forget-me-nots = I (2 strands, granitos), V (2 strands, colonial knot)

Construction

The shaded areas in the following diagrams indicate the right side of the fabric.

Cutting out

See the liftout pattern for the templates.

Order of work

Refer to the step-by-step instructions for working beaded Hedebo edge on page 83 and knotted pearl stitch on page 89.

1. Preparing the embroidered pieces

Block and press the embroidery following the instructions on page 37. Cut out along the marked cutting lines.

2. Preparing the front and back

Fuse a lightweight wadding piece to the wrong side of each embroidered

piece, aligning the edges with the tacking. Remove the tacking.

Apply a small amount of glue to one side of each plastic piece and attach a firm, medium weight wadding piece to each.

3. Preparing and attaching the lining

Fuse a piece of lightweight interfacing to the wrong side of each lining piece.

With right sides together and matching raw edges, machine stitch a lining piece to an embroidered piece along the lower straight edge (*diag 1*).

diag 1

Repeat for the remaining pieces.

4. Making the front and back

Secure a length of quilting thread in the seam allowance of the back piece and work gathering stitches around the entire edge of the combined cover and lining back piece, making the seam 2mm ($^1/_{16}$") wider on the sides of the lining (*diag 2*).

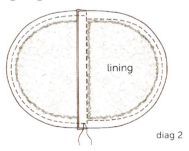

lining

diag 2

With the padded sides together, place a plastic piece over the wrong side of the embroidered front. Pull up the thread, gathering the seam allowance to the wrong side, over the plastic and secure (*diag 3*).

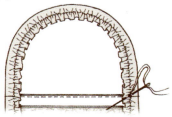

diag 3

Finger press the foldline between the embroidered piece and the lining. With wrong sides together, fold the lining over the back and ladder stitch to the seam allowance of the outer cover (*diag 4*).

diag 4

Repeat for the front.

5. Making the cover

Mark a 1.5cm (⁵⁄₈") opening at the centre top of one cover piece with pins (*diag 5*).

diag 5

Place the front and back cover with wrong sides together and matching edges. Ladder stitch the edges together using matching machine sewing thread, making sure to leave the opening free at the top.

Using three strands of O, work knotted pearl stitch over the seamline and along both sides of the opening at the top (*diag 6*).

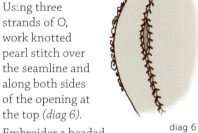

diag 6

Embroider a beaded Hedebo edge around the lower edge using two strands of the same thread and BP beads, keeping the cross stitches for the scallops approximately 6mm (¼") wide and the short stitches the width of a bead.

6. Making the twisted cord

Cut four 3m (3yd 10") lengths of X. Knot the threads together at each end and make a twisted cord. Secure a quilting thread to the folded end of the cord. Referring to the diagram, thread three beads onto the cord, take the cord through the opening in the cover from top to bottom, thread the thread cutter, then take the cord back up through the opening and thread the remaining three beads (*diag 7*).

diag 7

Determine the finished length of your cord to make the pendant hang at a comfortable length, and knot the folded end of the cord at the required measurement.

Loosely knot the cord inside each set of beads, approximately 4cm (1⁹⁄₁₆") from the knotted ends (*diag 8*).

diag 8

Overlap the ends of the cords, offsetting the knotted ends. Trim the tails at each end so the overlap measures 1cm (³⁄₈"). Stitch securely in place with matching machine sewing thread (*diag 9*).

7. Needlelace bead

Fuse a piece of appliqué paper to a piece of brown felt. Cut out a rectangle measuring 1cm x 4cm wide (³⁄₈" x 1⁹⁄₁₆") and peel off the backing paper. With the glue side uppermost, wrap the felt strip tightly around the knots. Stitch each end securely to the cord, pulling the stitches taut to round off the ends (*diag 10*).

diag 9   diag 10

Knot a strand of O and secure by sinking the knot into the felt roll. Work fourteen evenly spaced spokes around the felt cylinder, working each in the same direction by sliding the needle through the centre of the felt roll (*diag 11*).

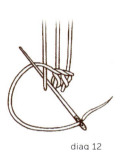

diag 11

Thread two 1m (40") strands of the same thread into the tapestry needle. Secure the thread inside the roll as before and emerge at one end. Work a blanket stitch over each spoke without picking up any felt (*diag 12*).

diag 12

When reaching the starting point, work the second round in detached blanket stitch, working a stitch into each stitch in the previous round without picking up the spokes. The spokes simply form a foundation for the first round of stitches (*diag 13*).

diag 13

Continue to cover the felt with rounds of detached blanket stitch, gradually increasing and decreasing the size of the stitches to accommodate the rounded ends of the bead. Secure the thread into the felt.

Slide the beads on one side close to the needlelace bead. Loosen the knot and reposition it firmly against the beads by placing the tip of a needle into the knot before tightening (*diag 14*).

diag 14

Repeat for the remaining side.

Step-by-step index

Armenian edging stitch

Armenian edging stitch is a knotted stitch that forms an attractive edge. It is most effective worked in a thick thread. Work from left to right to complete the stitch.

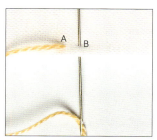

1. Emerge just above the finished edge at A. Take a small stitch from back to front over the edge at B.

2. Pull the thread through leaving a small loop. Twist the thread loop clockwise, forming a figure eight. Take the needle from back to front through the loop.

3. Pull the thread firmly away from the edge to form a knot. **Completed first stitch**.

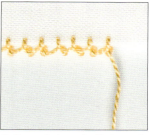

4. Repeat steps 1–3 at small intervals along the edge to the end of the row.

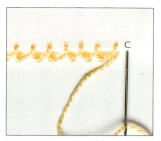

5. To finish, take the needle through the seam at C, a short distance from the last knot and secure the thread.

Beaded Hedebo edge

A Hedebo edge forms a decorative scalloped finish. A foundation of large and small cross stitches is embroidered first at the marked positions, and Hedebo stitch and beading are worked over this to form the scallops.

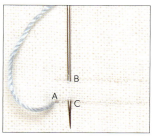

1. Bring the thread to the front at A. Take the needle to the back at B and emerge at C.

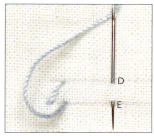

2. Pull the thread through. Take the needle from D to E.

3. Pull the thread through again. Take the needle from F to G. Pull the thread through.

4. Continue repeating steps 1–3. Take the thread to the back at H.

5. Bring thread to the front at I. Take the needle from J to K through previously used holes in the fabric.

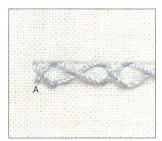

6. Pull the thread through. Continue working the remaining half of the cross stitches, finishing above A.

7. Bring the needle to the front at A, pick up a seed bead and take the needle to the back at B.

8. Pull the thread through and emerge at C. Slide the needle under the cross stitches keeping the thread over the needle.

9. Pull the thread through, until a small loop is formed. Take the needle through the loop as shown.

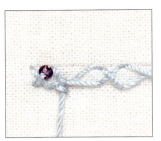

10. Pull the thread until the stitch sits snugly.

11. Repeat steps 8–10, packing the stitches closely so that a scallop is formed.

12. Take the needle to the back at D and emerge at E.

13. Pull the thread through and repeat steps 7–12 to complete the remaining scallops.

Cloud-filling stitch

This Jacobean stitch is an attractive filling technique. Use a fine tapestry needle for the lacing to avoid splitting the foundation stitches. We used contrasting threads for photographic purposes.

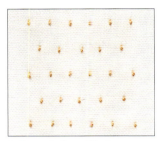

1. Foundation. Work a foundation of tiny straight stitches in a brick pattern. Space the stitches 3mm (1/8") apart and each row 5mm (3/16") apart.

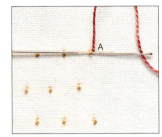

2. Lacing. Bring the thread to the front at A, just next to the first foundation stitch in the first row. Slide needle from right to left under the first foundation stitch.

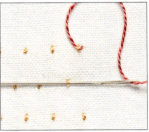

3. Gently pull the thread through. Slide the needle from right to left under the first stitch in the second row.

4. Pull the thread through gently. Slide the needle from right to left under the second stitch on the first row. Pull the thread through gently.

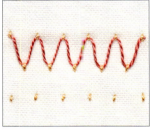

5. Continue in this manner to the end of the row, taking care not to pull the lacing thread too tight. Secure the thread at the back.

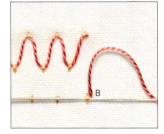

6. Bring a new thread to the front at B, next to the first foundation stitch on the third row. Slide the needle from right to left under the first stitch.

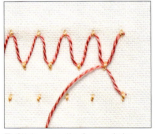

7. Slide needle from right to left under the first stitch on the second row, taking care not to split the previous lacing thread. Pull the thread through gently.

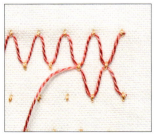

8. Lace under the second stitch on the third row and pull through. Slide the needle under the second stitch of the second row and pull through.

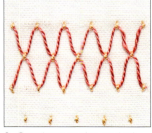

9. Continue to the end of the row in this manner. Take the thread to the back and secure.

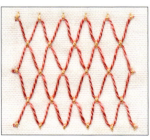

10. Continue to fill the shape with lacing in this manner.

Cretan stitch variation

Unlike regular Cretan stitch, each stitch is tied down individually in the counted stitch variation. Worked on evenweave fabric, each stitch is separated by a single fabric thread, however when using waste canvas, the vertical tie-down stitches are worked over a thread pair.

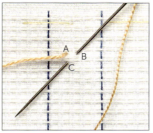

1. Bring the thread to the front at A. Take to the back at B, one thread pair to the right of A. Emerge at C, one thread pair below A.

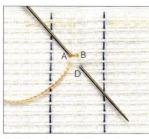

2. Take the needle to the back at A, and emerge at D, one thread pair below B.

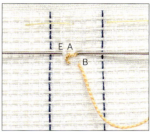

3. Take the needle to the back at B. Emerge at E, one thread to the left of A.

4. Take the needle to the back at F, one thread to the right of B. Emerge at G, one thread pair below C.

5. Take the needle to the back at C and emerge at H, one thread pair to the right of F.

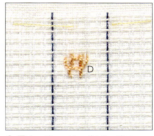

6. Take the needle to the back at D. Pull the thread through to complete the second stitch.

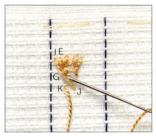

7. Emerge at I, one thread to the left of E. Take thread to the back at J and emerge at K, one thread pair below G. Take the needle to the back at G to anchor the stitch.

8. Emerge at L, one thread to the right of F. Take the thread to the back at K and emerge at J. Take the needle to the back at H to anchor the stitch.

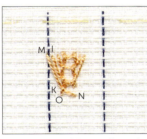

9. Emerge at M one thread to the left of I. Take the thread to the back at N, emerge at O and anchor the stitch at K.

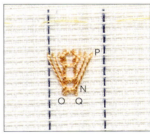

10. Work the following stitch from P to O, with the anchoring stitch from Q to N.

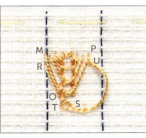

11. Stitch the next pair of stitches in a similar manner, working the first from R, one thread pair below M, to S, anchoring from T to O. Start the second from U, one thread pair below P.

12. Continue the row in this manner. Work diagonal satin stitches at each side to complete the row.

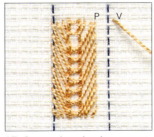

13. Second and subsequent rows. Bring the thread to the front at V, three threads to the right of P.

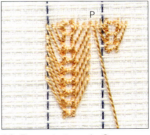

14. Repeat steps 1–8. Emerge at P.

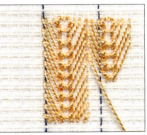

15. Repeat steps 9–12, working the left hand side of the row into the same holes as the right hand side of the previous row.

Eyelet for attaching shanks

These eyelets are worked larger than usual to allow the shanks of buttons or charms to sit neatly in the hole.

1. Start the thread with 2 or 3 tiny running stitches and trim the tail.

2. Work tiny back stitches around the edge of the circle. Split the first stitch to secure the thread.

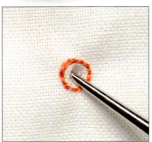

3. Use an awl or stiletto to pierce the centre of the circle.

4. Bring the thread to the front through the hole. Take the needle to the back just outside the back stitch line, angling the needle towards the centre.

5. Bring the thread to the front through the pierced hole and pull the thread taut away from the hole.

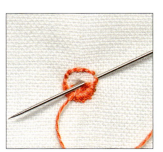

6. Work overcast stitch closely around the edge of the eyelet, taking the needle to the back outside the back stitch and emerging through the pierced hole.

WRONG SIDE

7. To finish, take the thread to the wrong side of the work and weave it under a few stitches on the back. Do not trim.

8. Attaching the shank. Ensuring the charm or button has the correct orientation, push the shank through the eyelet.

WRONG SIDE

9. Secure the charm or button by working 3 or 4 stitches through the shank, stitching into the back of the overcast stitches on each side of the eyelet. Secure the thread.

'Mid pleasures and palaces though we may roam,
Be it ever so humble, there's no place like home.

John Howard Payne

Glove stitch

Traditionally used in the making of fine kid gloves, this stitch is similar in appearance to a row of zigzag stitches. It is often used to join the edges of chatelaines or boxes, and makes a very pretty edge. Marking a line parallel to the edge will help to keep the stitches even.

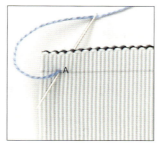

1. Bring the thread to the front at A. Take the thread over the edge and re-emerge at A.

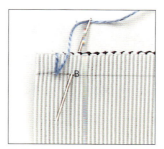

2. Pull the thread through to form a vertical straight stitch. Take the needle to the back and bring to the front at B.

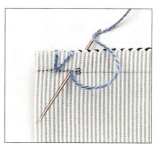

3. Pull the thread through, forming a diagonal straight stitch. Take the thread over the edge and re-emerge at B.

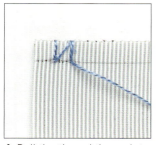

4. Pull the thread through to complete the zigzag.

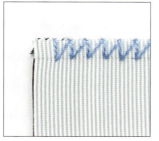

5. Continue in the same manner for the required distance, ending on a vertical stitch.

Hungarian braided chain stitch

This is worked in a similar manner to heavy chain stitch, but results in a more textured line. You might find it helpful to use the eye end of the needle to slide under the stitches.

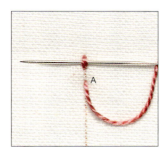

1. Work a tiny straight stitch at the end of the line. Emerge at A, a short distance from the first stitch, and slide the needle under the first stitch. Do not pierce the fabric.

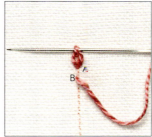

2. Pull the thread through and take the needle to the back at A. Emerge at B. Slide the needle under the straight stitch as before.

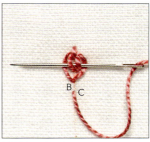

3. Take the thread to the back at B and emerge at C. The distance from B-C is the same as A-B. Slide the needle under the inside chain stitch only.

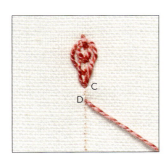

4. Pull the thread through. Take the thread to the back at C and emerge at D, an even distance from C.

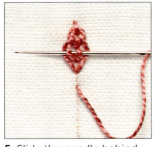

5. Slide the needle behind the innermost chain above as before.

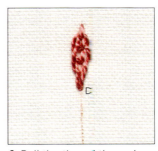

6. Pull the thread through and take the thread to the back at D.

7. Continue in this manner to the end of the row.

Interlaced chain stitch

This is an intricate variation of chain stitch that can make an attractive border or filling stitch. Use a tapestry needle for the interlacing to avoid splitting the previous stitches, and make sure to keep the interlacing stitches fairly loose. We used contrasting threads for photographic purposes.

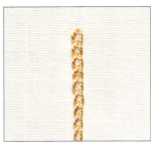

1. Foundation. Work a row of large chain stitches along the centre.

2. Interlacing. Bring a new thread to the front at the start of the chain stitch row. Slide the needle from the outside in, under the right hand side of the second chain stitch.

3. Pull thread through, laying the lacing thread along the outside of the chain. Slide the needle from the inside out under the right hand side of the first chain and under the lacing thread.

4. Pull thread through, so the lacing wraps loosely around the centre of the chains. Lace from the outside in, under the third chain. Pull the thread through gently so the thread rests outside the chain.

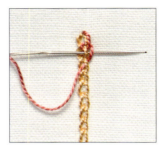

5. Slide the needle from the inside out, under the second chain and previous lacing.

6. Continue in this manner to the end of the row, ensuring the lacing rests along the outer edge of the chains and wraps neatly along the centre.

7. Bring a new thread to the front at the top of the row. Interlace the opposite side in a similar manner, ensuring the wraps lie neatly side by side along the centre.

Lacing and mitring corners over mountboard

This technique allows for fabric to be neatly secured over a solid surface such as mountboard. When lacing, check the front regularly to make sure it stays smooth. The corners are mitred once the lacing is complete.

1. Lacing. Press the seam allowances to the wrong side. Aligning the foldlines, fold and press the corners, taking care not to press out the previous foldlines.

2. With the wrong side facing, centre board over the wrong side of the fabric piece. Ensuring fabric is straight, pin in place at the midpoint along each side by pushing pins into the ends of the cardboard.

3. Thread a long length of doubled quilting thread into a sharps needle and knot the end. Secure the thread on one long edge of fabric, 2.5cm (1") from the board edge.

4. Work a 6mm (1/4") horizontal stitch through the overlapping fabric on the opposite edge. This reduces the stress to any one spot in the fabric.

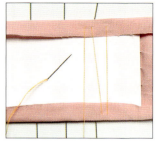

5. Pull the thread firmly. Work a 6mm (¼") stitch on the opposite side and pull firmly.

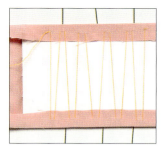

6. Continue in the same manner. Check the front is free from wrinkles as you work. Stop 2.5cm (1") from the opposite mountboard edge. Secure the thread, leaving a long tail.

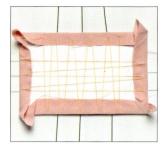

7. Lace the short ends in the same manner, starting and stopping 2.5cm (1") from the long edges of the fabric.

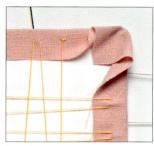

8. Mitring the corners. Fold the corner of the fabric to the wrong side.

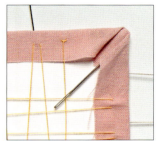

9. Holding the corner in place, use a darning needle to help tuck the corner in neatly, by sliding it between the layers.

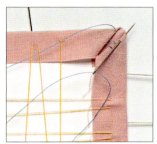

10. Secure the sewing thread 1cm (³/₈") from the corner and ladder stitch the mitre together towards the corner.

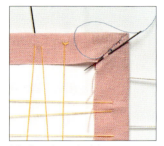

11. Continue ladder stitching down to the edge of the fabric to complete the mitre.

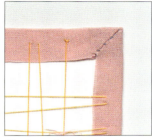

12. Completed mitred corner.

Knotted pearl stitch

This decorative stitch makes a perfect edging or attractive border. It is similar to Palestrina stitch, but worked from right to left rather than left to right. As well as edging and borders, it can also be worked in rows to form an interesting textured filling.

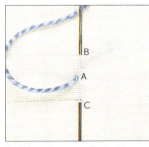

1. Bring the needle to the front at A. Take a stitch from B to C.

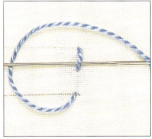

2. Pull the thread through. Slide the needle under the first stitch, ensuring the thread is under the tip of the needle.

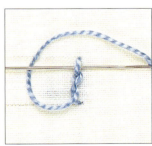

3. Pull the thread through to form a knot. Slide the needle under the first stitch, ensuring the thread is under the tip of the needle.

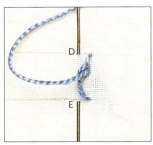

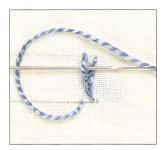

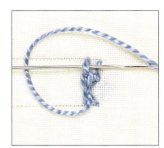

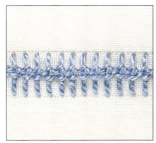

4. Pull the thread through. Insert the needle at D and emerge at E.

5. Pull the thread through. Slide the needle under the stitch, ensuring the thread is under the tip of the needle.

6. Pull the thread through and repeat for a second knot.

7. Continue in this manner for the required length.

Ladder stitch

Not to be confused with open chain stitch, or the ladder stitch used for construction. This is a very pretty, neat stitch that can be used to fill wide spaces. The raised knotted edges give an attractive finish.

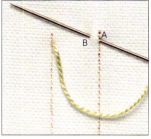

1. Bring thread to the front on the left hand side. Take it to back at A. Bring the needle to the front at B, just above and to the left of A.

2. Take the thread to the back at C just below A, and emerge at D, directly opposite C.

3. Holding the thread to the right, slide the needle under the left hand side of the first ladder stitch. Do not pierce the fabric.

4. Hold the thread below the stitch. Slide the needle from right to left under the right hand side of the first ladder and anchoring stitch.

5. Pull the thread through loosely. Take the needle to the back at E, just below the second ladder.

6. Bring the thread to the front at F. Holding the thread to the right, slide the needle under the left hand side of the second ladder.

7. Pull through loosely. Slide the needle under the right hand side of the second ladder and the previous wrap.

8. Take the needle to the back just below the wrapped ladder.

9. Continue in this manner to fill the space.

10. To create a curve, place the stitches close together at one side and further apart at the other.

Needlewoven picot

This picot is a lace-making technique used in stumpwork to create raised embroidery. The needlewoven picot is worked around a pin inserted in the fabric and is only attached to the fabric at one end. Beautiful picots depend on even tension and tightly packed stitches.

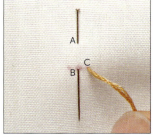

1. Foundation threads. Insert a long pin from A to B for 1cm (³/8"). This is the picot length. Bring thread to the front at C and pull through.

2. Wrap the thread anticlockwise under the head of the pin. Insert the needle at D.

3. Pull the thread through. Re-emerge just to the right of B. Pull the thread through.

4. Wrap the thread clockwise around the head of the pin. The centre thread crosses the pin and becomes the third foundation thread.

5. Holding the thread taut to the right. Give a firm tug.

6. Towards the top of the pin (A), weave the needle from right to left under the foundation threads (over, under, over).

7. Pull the thread through.

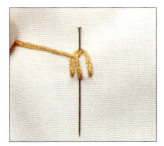

8. Pull the thread firmly up against the pin.

9. Holding thread taut to the left, weave needle from left to right (under, over, under) the foundation stitches. You may find it easier to turn the work slightly to do this.

10. Pull the thread through until the loop is snug against the first foundation thread.

11. Weave the needle from right to left under the centre thread. Push needle up towards the top of the picot. Pack the threads as tightly as possible.

12. Begin to pull the thread through.

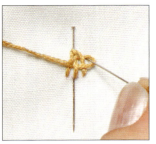

13. Before the thread is completely through, place point of needle in the loop being formed. (This helps to maintain the shape, keeping the outer line of foundation threads even).

14. Weave from left to right, sliding needle under, over, under (step 9). Continue weaving towards the base of the picot, packing firmly each left-to-right row.

15. Continue weaving until the foundation threads are firmly packed. Take the needle to the back at the base of the picot (close to C).

16. Pull through and end off on the wrong side Remove the pin. **Completed picot.** The picot can now be twisted and manipulated into shape.

Palestrina knot

Also known as old English knot, Smyrna stitch, double knot stitch and tied coral stitch, Palestrina knot produces a line of raised knots useful for outlines or borders.
It is important that the knots are evenly spaced and close together.

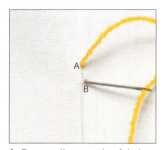

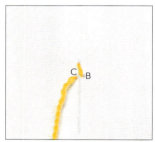

1. Draw a line on the fabric. Bring needle to front at A, at the top of the line. Take needle to back at B, just to the right of the line and 4mm (3/16") away from A.

2. Bring the needle to the front at C, to the left of the line and opposite B. Pull the thread through.

3. Slide the needle under the first stitch from right to left with the needle pointing upwards. Do not go through the fabric.

4. Begin to pull the thread through.

5. Continue pulling the thread through gently until the loop hugs the straight stitch.

6. Make a loop to the left.

7. Slide the needle from right to left under thread as shown. Emerge between B and C. Do not pierce the fabric. Ensure loop is under needle tip.

8. Gently pull the thread through forming a soft knot. **Completed first knot.**

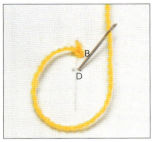

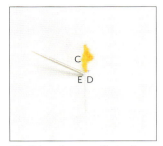

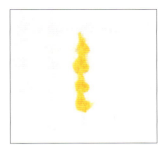

9. To begin the second stitch, take the needle to the back at D, a short distance below B.

10. Bring the needle to the front at E, just to the left of the line (opposite D, below C).

11. Complete the stitch following steps 3–8.

12. Continue working stitches in the same manner. End off by taking needle to the back, close to the base of the last stitch. **Completed Palestrina knot.**

Portuguese border stitch

This stitch forms an attractive raised braid. It makes a heavy edge, or can be used as a filling stitch. The angle of the foundation stitches can be changed to create a curved stitch. Use a fine tapestry needle for the lacing to avoid splitting the foundation stitches.

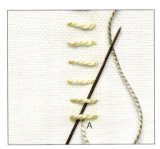

1. Foundation. Work a vertical row of even straight stitches for the foundation, spacing the stitches 3mm (1/8") apart.

2. Lacing, first pass. Bring the thread to the front at A, below the the first foundation stitch. Holding the thread to the right, slide the needle towards you under the first two foundation stitches without piercing the fabric.

3. Gently pull the thread through, taking care not to distort the foundation stitches. Hold the thread to the right and slide it under stitch 2, to the left of the first lacing stitch. Pull the thread through gently.

4. Holding the thread to the right, slide the needle under stitches 3 and 2, to the left of the previous lacing stitches.

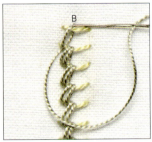

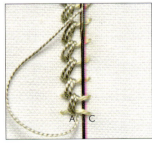

5. Hold the thread to the right and slide the needle under stitch 3 again. Keeping the thread to the right, slide the needle under stitches 4 and 3.

6. Pull the thread through. Continue in this manner to the top of the row. Take the needle to the back at B, just above the last foundation stitch.

7. Lacing, second pass. Bring the thread to the front at C, just next to A. Holding the thread to the left, slide the needle under stitches 2 and 1. Pull through gently.

8. Keeping the thread to the left, slide the needle under stitch 2. Hold the thread to the left and slide the needle towards you under stitches 3 and 2.

9. Pull through gently and slide the needle under stitch 3. With the thread to the left, slide the needle under stitches 4 and 3.

10. Continue in this manner to the top of the row. Take the needle to the back at D, just above the last foundation stitch.

Portuguese knotted stem stitch

Portuguese knotted stem stitch, also known simply as Portuguese stem stitch, is an attractive outline stitch. It can also be worked as a filling stitch of side-by-side rows, with the knots alternating position.

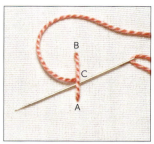

1. Work a stitch from A to B. Bring the needle to the front at C. With the thread above the needle, slide the needle from right to left under the stitch, below C.

2. Gently begin to pull the thread through.

3. Continue pulling thread through. Pull upwards towards C, so a wrap is formed over the first stitch.

4. Keeping the thread above the needle, slide the needle under the first stitch again and below the first wrap.

5. Pull the thread through so a second wrap is formed below the first.

6. To begin the second stem stitch, take the needle to the back at D.

7. Pull the thread through.

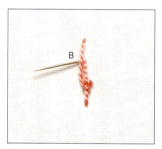

8. Bring the needle to the front at B, to the left of the second stem stitch.

9. Keeping the thread above, slide the needle from right to left under the first and second stem stitches below B.

10. Pull the thread through. Keeping the thread above the needle, slide the needle from right to left under the wrap just formed.

11. Pull the thread through so a second wrap is formed.

12. Continue working in the same manner. To end, take the needle to the back under the last wrap and secure.

Raised cross stitch

This stitch forms a flower worked over the four spokes created by an upright cross. We used no. 5 perlé cotton for photographic purposes.

1. Work an upright cross stitch. Bring the needle to the front at A at the centre, just below and to the right of the cross.

2. Take the needle under the right spoke, without picking up any fabric. Keep the thread under the needle tip.

3. Pull the thread through, around the spoke of the cross.

4. Turn the fabric 90 degrees to the right. Take the needle under the next spoke in the same manner.

5. Work over the remaining spokes, turning the fabric for each stitch. Ensure the stitches lie closely around the centre. **Completed first round.**

6. Continue in this manner around the spokes until the cross is covered. Take the needle under the weaving and secure. **Completed raised cross stitch.**

Rococo stitch variation

This variation of rococo stitch produces more elongated stitches than the regular rococo stitch. Interlocking rows of rococo stitch make an excellent textured filling. It is best worked on counted thread fabric. If working in a hoop, work the stitches in a stabbing motion.

1. Bring the thread to the front at A. Take the thread to the back at B, eight fabric threads below. Emerge at C, four threads above and one thread to the right of B.

2. Take the needle to the back at D, two threads to the left of C and re-emerge at A.

3. Keeping the thread to the left, take the needle to back at B and re-emerge at D.

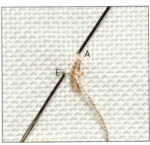

4. Take the needle to the back at E, two threads to the left of D and re-emerge at A.

5. Keeping the thread to the right, take the needle to the back at B and re-emerge at C.

6. Take the needle to the back at F, two threads to the right of C to complete the first stitch.

7. Bring the thread to the front at G, six threads to the right of A.

8. Work the second stitch in the same manner as before.

9. Continue in this manner to complete the row.

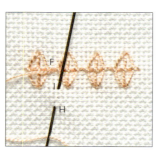

10. Subsequent rows. Bring thread to the front at F and take it to the back H, eight threads below F. Emerge at I, four threads above and one to the right of H.

11. Complete the stitch following steps 2–6.

12. Continue to fill the shape with rows in this manner, adjusting the width and direction of the outermost stitches to follow a curved outline.

Rosette stitch

These roses are a quick and effective way to add variety to floral embroidery. The needle is inserted into the fabric to form the framework around which the thread is wound. After winding, the thread is couched in place.

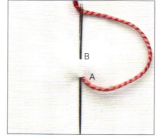

1. Bring the needle to the front at A. Insert the needle at B, 3mm (1/8") above A. Re-emerge at A. Leave the needle in the fabric.

2. Pick up the thread at A. Wrap the thread under each end of the needle in a counter clockwise direction.

3. Work 2–3 more wraps in the same manner. Ensure the wraps lie side by side and not on top of each other.

4. Holding the wraps in place with your left thumb near the top, gently pull the needle through.

5. Still holding the wraps with your thumb, take the thread over the wraps and to the back of the fabric.

6. Pull the thread through. Bring the needle to the front at the top, inside the last wrap.

7. Take the needle to the back over the last wrap and pull the thread through.

Threaded satin stitch honeycomb

This counted thread stitch creates a textured filling, perfectly imitating the ridges of roof tiles. Satin stitch is worked in blocks of six stitches over four fabric threads in diagonal rows across the linen. We used contrasting threads for photographic purposes.

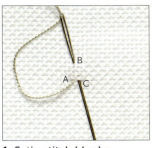

1. Satin stitch blocks. Emerge at A. Take the needle to the back at B, four fabric threads above and emerge at C, one thread to the right of A.

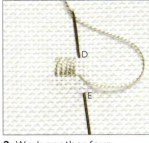

2. Work another four stitches in this manner. Take the needle to the back at D and emerge at E, one thread to the right and eight threads below D.

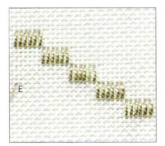

3. Repeat steps 1 and 2 diagonally across the shape. Emerge at E, eight threads below the first block above.

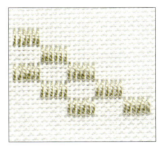

4. Stitch a diagonal row of satin stitch blocks, each six stitches wide over four fabric threads in the same manner as before.

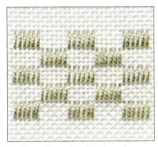

5. Continue to fill the shape in this manner.

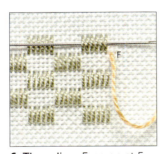

6. Threading. Emerge at F, one thread to the right of the outermost block. Slide the needle under the first block of satin stitches.

7. Pull the thread through. Slide the needle under the first block in the row below.

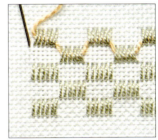

8. Repeat to the end of the row. Take the needle to the back one thread to the left of the outermost block.

9. Emerge at G, four threads below F. Slide the needle under the first block as before.

10. Lace the thread back through the second and third rows of blocks in a similar manner and take to the back.

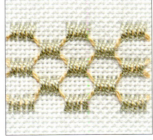

11. Continue to lace rows of thread into the blocks in this manner to fill the shape.

Trellis stitch

Trellis stitch is a needlelace filling stitch that was very popular in the seventeenth century. It is a detached stitch, anchored into a row of foundation stitches along the outer edges. The size of the foundation stitches outlining the shape will determine the effect of the trellis stitch filling.

Use a fine tapestry needle for the trellis stitch to avoid splitting the foundation stitches. We used contrasting threads for photographic purposes.

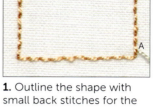

1. Outline the shape with small back stitches for the foundation. Bring the needle to the front at A, just outside the lower right hand edge of the foundation.

2. Slide the needle from top to bottom under the first foundation stitch to the left of A.

3. Begin to pull the thread through, leaving a small loop above the foundation stitch. Hold the thread to the right and slide the needle under the loop from top to bottom.

4. Pull the thread through. Pull the loop to the left then to the right to form a firm knot.

5. Repeat steps 2–4 into each foundation stitch, pulling each stitch first to the left then to the right to tighten. At the end of the row, slide the needle from left to right to anchor the row.

6. Slide the needle under the back stitch above in the same direction and pull the thread through to begin the second row.

7. Slide the needle from top to bottom under the loop between the last two knots on the previous row.

8. Begin to pull the thread through, leaving a small loop. Hold the thread to the right and slide the needle through the loop from top to bottom.

9. Pull the thread to the right, then to the left to tighten the knot.

10. Continue to the end of the row, working into each loop in the previous row in this manner.

HINTS *Trellis stitch*

To tighten each knot always pull the thread in the direction you are stitching before pulling it back towards the last stitch.

To increase, work the first trellis stitch under the loop between the foundation stitch and the last knot in the previous row.

To decrease, work the first trellis stitch under the second loop of the previous row.

Tighten the knot, pulling in the direction of the missed stitch to close the gap.

11. Anchor the row, sliding the needle from right to left under the back stitch at the opposite side. Slide the needle under the back stitch above.

12. Continue to fill the shape in the same manner.

13. To anchor the last row, work the stitches into the foundation stitches along the upper edge

Up and down blanket stitch loop

This stitch prevents loops from twisting. The foundation of the loop should be a little tighter than the finished requirement as the loop stretches slightly when covered. We used contrasting threads for photographic purposes.

1. Work three parallel straight stitches for the foundation of the loop. Bring a new thread to the front at the right hand side of the foundation stitches.

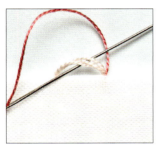

2. With the tip pointing away from you, take the needle under the loop, keeping the working thread under the tip of the needle.

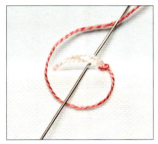

3. Pull the thread through, pulling the stitch firmly around the foundation. Loop the thread downwards. With the tip pointing towards you, take the needle under the loop, keeping the thread under the tip.

4. Pull the thread through towards you.

5. Pull the thread to the right, forming a small knot on the outer edge of the loop.

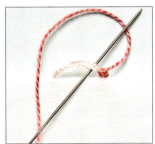

6. Work the next stitch around the loop with the tip of the needle pointing away.

7. Work the fourth stitch, looping the working thread downwards and with the needle tip pointing towards you.

8. Complete to covering the foundation loop in this manner, pushing the stitches close together.

WELCOME
Home